VOLUME

54

The New York Times

DAILY CROSSWORD PUZZLES

Edited by
Will Shortz

**Random House
Puzzles & Games**

SOLUTIONS TO THE PUZZLES ARE
FOUND AT THE BACK OF THE BOOK.

———————

Random House Puzzles & Games Web site address:
www.puzzlesatrandom.com

Text design by Julia Reynolds, Stanley Newman and Mark Frnka
Typography by Mark Frnka
Manufactured in the United States of America
4 5 6 7 8 9 10

Introduction

Crosswords are by nature a solitary activity—a battle between you and the puzzlemaker conducted via the printed page (or, now, a computer screen), which each side does by himself.

But today more and more solvers seem to be finding a social side to puzzling as well.

One couple I know solves *The New York Times* crossword together in bed before going to sleep. On an easy puzzle they play competitively, alternating answers, each building off the previous answer of the other person (if a crossing answer is open). For a tough puzzle they pool their efforts.

From telephone calls and letters I know that lots of you do the *Times* puzzle at work with your officemates. Presumably, this is done during breaks . . . but I don't want to ask!

On Sunday the long-distance phone lines hum as far-flung family members swap hints on the Sunday puzzle—or gloat over the answers they have that their opposites don't.

And now with the Internet, many of you are getting connected on-line. *The New York Times* conducts an electronic crossword forum, for example, through which you can post and read messages to and from other solvers about the puzzles. Ask questions about answers you don't understand, discuss the clues, share your solving strategies and hang-ups. Many long distance friendships have been started in this way. In case you're interested, the website is at <www.nytimes.com>. Follow the links to Forums → Diversions → Crossword Talk. Registration is required, but free.

Meanwhile, here is a brand-new collection of 50 crosswords from the daily *New York Times*. For the first time in this series, all the puzzles are of medium difficulty (that is, selected from Tuesday, Wednesday, and Thursday newspapers). The easier puzzles (Monday) and harder puzzles (Friday and Saturday) now appear in volumes all their own, so you can choose exactly the difficulty level you like the most.

Feel free to solve the puzzles by yourself, or share them with a friend!

—Will Shortz

1 QUITE UPSET by Gerald R. Ferguson

ACROSS

1 Pickle container
4 Motionless
9 Fashion
14 Matriarch of all matriarchs
15 Actor Romero
16 Boiling
17 Weighed in
20 Light lunches
21 To any extent
22 List-ending abbr.
23 Moo juice container
25 Grp. overseeing toxic cleanups
28 Perfect rating
29 Most prudent
31 Become raveled
32 Painful spots
33 Carroll adventuress
34 Caused disharmony
38 Napping spots
39 Magazine exhortation
40 Break in relations
41 Out of business
43 Compaq products
46 __ Miss
47 Engulfs in amusement
48 Cream ingredient
49 Tear to shreds
51 Part of MOMA
53 Blabbed
57 __ pedis (athlete's foot)
58 Take to the stump
59 Certain shirt
60 Anxiety
61 Wanderer
62 Japanese honorific

DOWN

1 High-fliers
2 Fly
3 Change tactics
4 Like an éclair
5 Composer Rorem and others
6 Superlative ending
7 Short cheer
8 Firestone features
9 Clergyman
10 Kind of surgery
11 Indoor court
12 Indian with a bear dance
13 Some M.I.T. grads
18 Chum
19 Leave be
23 Wielded
24 Partner of search
26 Warsaw __
27 Word of assent
29 Canton cookware
30 Land west of Eng.
31 Current
32 Sing "shooby-doo"
33 Out for the night
34 Aggravate
35 Part of a church service
36 Piano-playing Dame
37 Ariz.-to-Kan. dir.
38 Sign of stage success
41 Professor Plum's game
42 Pomeranian, for one
43 Stitched folds
44 Window of an eye
45 Breath mint brand
47 Sloppy landing sound
48 Suffix with stock
50 France's __ de Glénans
51 Queens team
52 Follow the code
53 __ Puf fabric softener
54 Wrestler's goal
55 Have a go at
56 Gen. Arnold of W.W. II fame

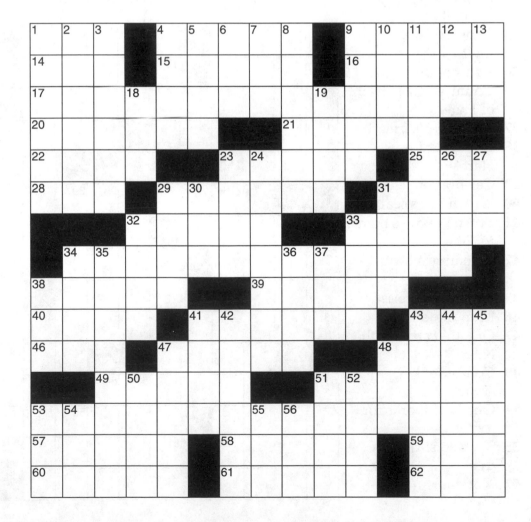

ACROSS

1 Some sports cars, for short
5 Foundation
10 Yield
14 Grimm villain
15 Novelist Jong
16 Jump at the Ice Capades
17 British heavy metal group
19 Canned meat brand
20 Disney's Dwarfs, e.g.
21 Printings
23 Support for Tiger Woods?
24 Pop singer Peeples
26 Prepares leather
27 Do a few odd jobs
32 __ Ababa
35 Cape Cod resort town
36 Acuff of the Country Music Hall of Fame
37 Androcles's friend
38 Headgear for Hardy
39 Celebration
40 Worshiper's seat
41 Bruce Wayne's home, for one
42 Valentine's Day gift
43 Inexpert motorist
46 Klondike strike
47 Org. that advises the N.S.C.
48 Computer key abbr.
51 One who works for a spell?
55 Sautéed shrimp dish
57 Not this

58 Huck Finn portrayer, 1993
60 Bring to ruin
61 As a companion
62 To be, in Tours
63 Afrikaner
64 London length
65 Fortune-teller

DOWN

1 Ceiling supporter
2 Conform (with)
3 Search blindly
4 E-mailed
5 "Hit the bricks!"
6 Jackie's second
7 Pro or con
8 Chilled the Chablis
9 Hygienic

10 Dealer's employer
11 Film box datum
12 Cain of "Lois & Clark"
13 Stately shaders
18 Luncheonette lists
22 Tropical root
25 Look after, with "to"
27 Wrestler's goal
28 Diamond flaw?
29 Decorative heading
30 Bit of marginalia
31 Changes color, in a way
32 European chain
33 The Almighty, in Alsace
34 Reduce in rank

38 Class distraction
39 On behalf of
41 Having a Y chromosome
42 Boxer's stat
44 Alter deceptively
45 Countenance
48 Overplay onstage
49 Fern fruit
50 Autumn beverage
51 Hit, as the toe
52 "You gotta be kidding!"
53 Model MacPherson
54 Very funny fellow
56 Makes one's jaw drop
59 Dad's namesake: Abbr.

3) AU PAIR by Fred Piscop

ACROSS

1 Scores for the Maple Leafs
6 Heavyweight champ dethroned by Braddock
10 In this way
14 Hold, as the attention
15 Any of three English rivers
16 Wax's opposite
17 In solitary
18 Dressed
19 As before, in footnotes
20 Batman and Robin, e.g.
22 Evening, informally
23 G.I. dinner
24 Kitty __
26 Where to find Chile powder?
29 Vinegar: Prefix
31 Statement of belief
32 Obliquely
36 Diamond Head locale
37 Kind of mill
38 Within: Prefix
39 It's about thyme!
41 Impels
42 Expunge
43 Miniature map
44 50's-60's pitcher Don
47 Einstein's birthplace
48 Declare
49 Tinker-Evers-Chance forte
56 New Zealander
57 Cartoonist Peter
58 Tylenol competitor
59 Mideast carrier
60 __ Hari
61 Wouk work
62 Beach, basically
63 Kind of car
64 Handle a baton

DOWN

1 Mortarboard wearer
2 Overly smooth
3 View from Stratford
4 Horne who sang " 'Deed I Do"
5 Restrained, as a flow
6 Game with wooden balls
7 "__ Lang Syne"
8 Jacob's twin
9 Aromatic
10 Prominent Manhattan sight
11 Equestrian's garb
12 Bring together
13 Jewish feast
21 Apr. payee
25 Communications corp.
26 Give __ (care)
27 Royal Crown Cola brand
28 Condition in kids' card games
29 __ B. Toklas
30 Amontillado holder
31 Subjects for Barron's: Abbr.
32 Sp. ladies
33 "Picnic" writer
34 Manuscript mark
35 Dawn goddess
37 Sporty Pontiacs
40 Palindromic preposition
41 Not intentional
43 "Well, __ be!"
44 Aral and Caspian Seas, really
45 Spanish tourist center
46 "Laugh-In" co-host
47 W.W. II predator
50 Kind of thermometer
51 Biblical preposition
52 Farm need
53 __ Strauss jeans
54 Swear
55 "Gimme a C . . . !" is one

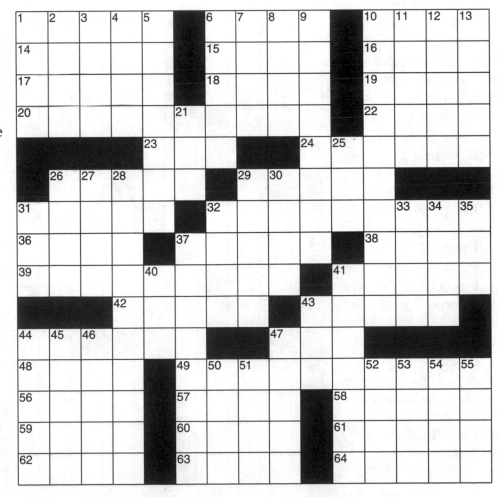

SPHERES OF INFLUENCE *by Gregory E. Paul*

ACROSS

1 Cobblers
5 City near Phoenix
10 "Half-Breed" singer
14 Med. sch. course
15 All possible
16 Part of A.P.R.
17 Nimble
18 Dancer Jeanmaire
19 Persia, today
20 The Boy King
21 Sculpture in the Louvre
23 Madalyn O'Hair, e.g.
25 "Norma __"
26 Deborah's role in "The King and I"
27 Reason for a small craft advisory
32 Paris newspaper, with "Le"
34 Blow one's top
35 Circle segment
36 Baker's dozen
37 Sign of spring
38 Headliner
39 What Dorian Gray didn't do
40 "__ Irish Rose"
41 Computer device
42 Dogpatch dweller
44 Author John Dickson __
45 Bill's partner
46 Costa Rican export
49 Former Ford offering
54 Org. that sticks to its guns
55 Bread spread
56 Memorable ship
57 Count calories
58 Gen. Bradley
59 Modify
60 __ Domini

61 Precious metal
62 Lascivious looks
63 He was a "Giant" star

DOWN

1 Naples noodles
2 Enter, as data
3 1955 hit for the Penguins
4 Pig's digs
5 Mother __
6 The Super Bowl, e.g.
7 Diner's card
8 Nov. electee
9 Tears?
10 "__ and Misdemeanors"
11 Mata __
12 Useful Latin abbr.
13 Gambler's mecca
21 Ivy plant
22 It may be Far or Near
24 Brings to a close
27 Town __ (early newsman)
28 Regrets
29 Apollo mission
30 Intervals of history
31 Farm measure
32 Repast
33 Today, in Turin
34 Southernmost Great Lake

37 Irregular
38 Carolina rail
40 "__ Ben Adhem" (Leigh Hunt poem)
41 Tailless cat
43 International agreement
44 Wickerworkers
46 Sketch comic John
47 Sports center
48 Squelched
49 Synthesizer man
50 "Tickle Me" doll
51 Genuine
52 Where Bill met Hillary
53 Lo-fat
57 Father figure

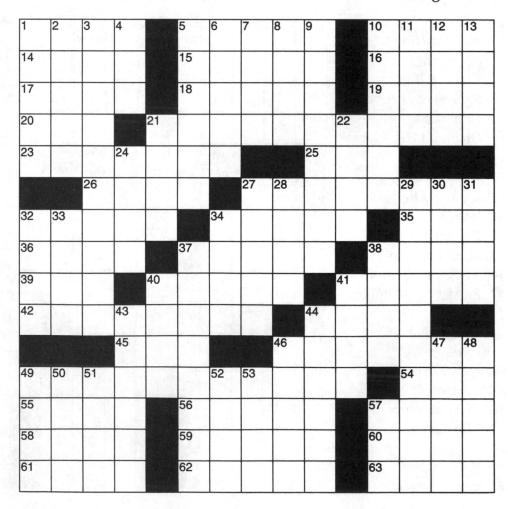

NOT ALL THERE by Elizabeth C. Gorski

ACROSS

1 "Let's go!"
5 Miss Cinders of old comics
9 Stravinsky's "Le __ du printemps"
14 It's pulled on a pulley
15 Music for two
16 Farm units
17 Once more
18 Schooner part
19 Signified
20 NBC comedy
23 Passing grade
24 Director Howard
25 X's in bowling
27 It's behind home plate
32 Sugar source
33 "__ American Cousin" (1858 play)
34 Results of big hits?
36 "Gandhi" setting
39 Egyptian, e.g.
41 1997 has two
43 Brothers and sisters
44 Flattens
46 Plains home
48 Tam-o'-shanter
49 Yin's counterpart
51 Not the subs
53 Liberace wore them
56 A.F.L.'s partner
57 Tempe sch.
58 Novelty timepiece
64 Cinnamon unit
66 __-Seltzer
67 First name in supermodeldom
68 Actress Berry
69 Alice doesn't work here anymore
70 Campus authority
71 Buzzing
72 Organic fuel
73 Klutz's utterance

DOWN

1 Pack in
2 "__ Lisa"
3 Like a William Safire piece
4 Alternative to J.F.K. and La Guardia
5 Oilers' home
6 Molokai meal
7 For fear that
8 Esqs.
9 Belushi character on "S.N.L."
10 Expert
11 Bartender's supply
12 "Walk Away __" (1966 hit)
13 __ Park, Colo.
21 Pear type
22 Like some stocks, for short
26 Lodges
27 Part of an old English Christmas feast
28 Atmosphere
29 Hodgepodge
30 Cross out
31 Glazier's items
35 Back-to-school time: Abbr.
37 Building support
38 Egyptian threats
40 Romeo
42 Maine's is rocky
45 Tee-hee
47 Psychiatrist Berne
50 Bearded creature
52 "Holy __!"
53 Russian-born violinist Schneider, informally
54 These, in Madrid
55 Rascal
59 "Twittering Machine" artist
60 Neighbor of Kan.
61 Nondairy spread
62 Bit of thunder
63 Dolls since 1961
65 Cato's 151

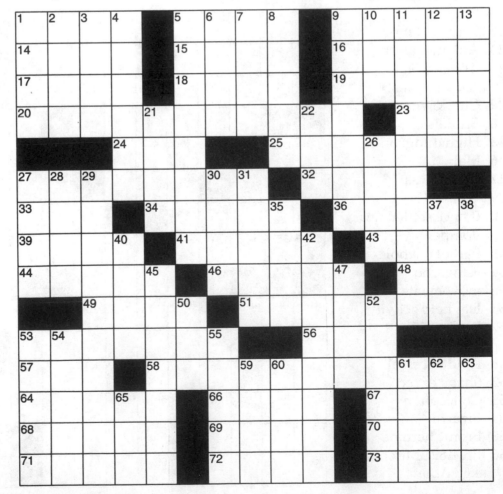

ACROSS

1 Certain drapes
6 Atlantic food fish
10 Gator's kin
14 Cop __ (confess for a lighter sentence)
15 White-tailed flier
16 Deli offering
17 Colt 45, e.g.
19 List member
20 "That's a lie!"
21 Household
23 70's-80's robotic rock group
25 The United States, metaphorically
27 Uris hero
28 Dance, in Dijon
29 Member of the 500 HR club
30 Rock impresario Brian
31 Surgical fabric
33 Ant, in dialect
35 "Texaco Star Theater" host
39 Cut down
40 Brilliance
43 High dudgeon
46 Mai __
47 Go on to say
49 "Bravo!"
50 It once settled near Pompeii
53 Part of a whole
54 Kangaroo movements
55 Hayfield activity
57 Prefix with China
58 Kind of cereal
62 Shade of red
63 Conception
64 Bizarre
65 Brontë heroine
66 Pre-1821 Missouri, e.g.: Abbr.

67 He had Scarlett fever

DOWN

1 Uncle of note
2 New Deal prog.
3 Stream deposit
4 "I can't __" (Stones refrain)
5 Morton product
6 "Rocky II," e.g.
7 Diabolical
8 Due halved
9 Words of assistance
10 "I __" (ancient Chinese text)
11 Record again
12 Where to find Eugene

13 Awaken
18 Early Shirley role
22 Signed up for
23 U.N.'s Hammarskjöld
24 Former polit. cause
26 __ of the Unknowns
28 Like some greeting cards
32 Nine-digit number, maybe
33 Ultimate point
34 R.N.'s offering
36 Send
37 Trompe l'__
38 Stretch
41 He KO'd Quarry, 10/26/70

42 Asian holiday
43 Tipple
44 "Didja ever wonder . . . ?" humorist
45 Successful escapee
47 Incarnation
48 Spanish Surrealist
51 Certain investment, informally
52 More competent
53 Jesse who lost to Ronald Reagan in 1970
56 Composer Stravinsky
59 Ending with quiet
60 N.Y.C. subway
61 Modern information source, with "the"

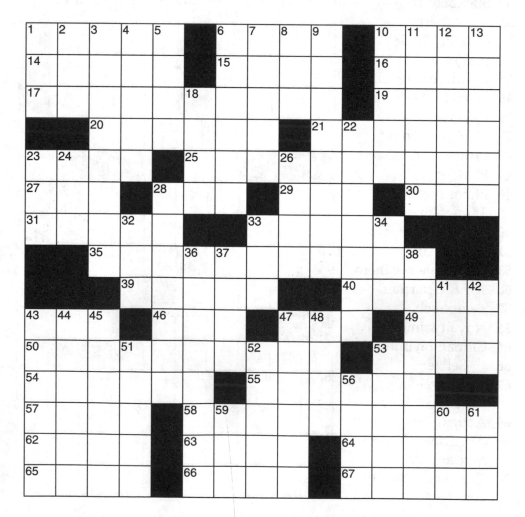

CHOICE WORDS by John R. Conrad

ACROSS

1 Smart
5 Diminished by
10 E, in Morse code
13 Nimbus
14 Makes amends (for)
16 Morn's opposite
17 Part of B.P.O.E.
18 Like some regions
19 Levy
20 No middle ground, successwise
23 Corn serving
24 Mornings, for short
25 Like some history
28 "Beau __"
31 Not guzzle
32 __ firma
33 Sounds from the stands
34 Approximately
36 Trial judge Lance
37 Dad's mate
38 Bit of hope
39 Turndowns
40 Words before taking the plunge
43 Certain breakout
44 Channels
45 Married
46 Newspapers
47 At bats, e.g.
48 Eternal queen, of book and film
49 Former Mideast merger: Abbr.
50 Eventually
56 Hawaiian necklace
58 __ to go (eager)
59 The Clintons' alma mater
60 Possess
61 Pindar's country
62 Class with a Paul Samuelson text
63 Entreat
64 Pothook shapes
65 1958 Presley #1 hit

DOWN

1 One whose work causes a stir?
2 Robust
3 Actress Chase
4 Pampers
5 Estate home
6 Anatomical passage
7 Foul
8 Free
9 Appears
10 Hoped-for effect of having a big military
11 Eggs
12 Cowhand's nickname
15 __ Lanka
21 __ kwon do
22 Christmas carol
26 Cases for insurance detectives
27 Maidens
28 Operates, as a hand organ
29 Patronize restaurants
30 Highlighting
31 In an undetermined place, in dialect
32 Attempt
34 Back-to-work time: Abbr.
35 Paddle
37 __ Olson (ad character)
41 Director Preminger
42 Eastern thrushes
43 In formation
46 Buddy
48 Trap
49 Prods
51 Assoc.
52 A long time ago
53 Sandwich with fixin's
54 Carolina college
55 1996 Tony musical
56 High return
57 Farm mother

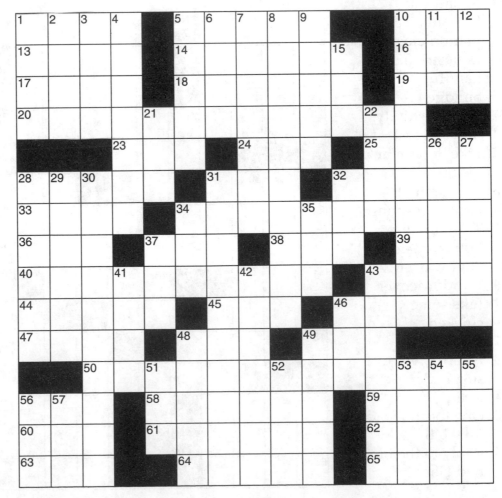

ACROSS

1 It's hailed by city dwellers
5 "The final frontier"
10 Philosopher David
14 Plow pullers
15 Director Welles
16 Ukraine's Sea of __
17 One socially challenged
18 Scottish estate owner
19 "Oh, my!"
20 Bad news
23 Philosopher John
24 It comes from the heart
28 Tampa neighbor, informally
31 Maladroit
33 "Common Sense" pamphleteer
34 Equestrian's handful
36 Smidgen
37 Lots of activity
41 Baseball stat
42 Like Superman's vision
43 Less tanned
44 Kickoff response
47 TV journalist Poussaint et al.
48 Highway curves
49 Window cover
51 Like some chicken
57 Talk
60 Alternatives to suspenders
61 Keen
62 One for the road
63 $100 bill
64 Reply to the Little Red Hen

65 "That was a close one!"
66 Planted
67 Word with high or hole

DOWN

1 Chinese secret society
2 Skater's move
3 Dry: Prefix
4 Slothful
5 Comfort giver
6 Short-sheeting a bed, e.g.
7 Stage remark
8 Part of a parachute
9 Prefix with -morph
10 Upper part of a barn
11 Terrorist's weapon
12 Swab
13 "The Three Faces of __"
21 "Psycho" setting
22 Sturdy furniture material
25 Tot's noisemaker
26 Rose's home, in song
27 Common vipers
28 Globe
29 Ford model
30 Galileo's kinsmen
31 Amos's partner
32 Part of "www"
34 Luke preceder

35 Santa __, Calif.
38 First-rate: Abbr.
39 Flip over
40 Shoal
45 Confer (upon)
46 Volcano detritus
47 Got the suds out
49 "Look out __!"
50 Starbucks serving
52 Kindergarten instruction
53 Gambling game
54 The Bard's river
55 Toy with a tail
56 Singer Brickell
57 Beret
58 "Come again?"
59 Noshed

9 JACKS OF ALL TRADES by Fred Piscop

ACROSS

1 Singer-actress Lane
5 "__ Mia" (1965 hit)
9 Choreographer Agnes de __
14 Watery
15 Stratford-Avon link
16 Firefighter Red
17 TV/film actor Jack
19 Comparatively modern
20 Scott's "__ Roy"
21 Got a move on
22 Honeybunch
23 Humdingers
25 Octave followers, in sonnets
28 It's hoisted in a pub
29 T'ai __ ch'uan
30 Phillips University site
31 Writer Jack
34 Form 1040 completer
35 Scourge
38 Idolize
39 Escritoire
40 "Boola Boola" singer
41 Pugilist Jack
43 Savoir-faire
45 Skater Midori
46 Superaggressive one
50 Barrow residents
52 Licked boots?
54 Grasslands
55 Crash diet
56 Absorbed, as an expense
57 AOL memos
59 Movie actor Jack
61 Haggard
62 "Garfield" dog
63 Grid coach __ Alonzo Stagg
64 Loquacious, in slang
65 Kind of blocker
66 Sit in the sun

DOWN

1 Oscar and Obie
2 Wisconsin college
3 Psycho talk?
4 Manage to get, with "out"
5 Doll
6 Church recesses
7 Crucifix
8 Gloucester's cape
9 They're combed on a farm
10 Imagine
11 Lyricist Jack
12 "The check is in the mail," maybe
13 Blow it
18 Kind of wine
22 Clears for takeoff?
24 Word of Valleyspeak
25 High-pitched
26 Much of a waiter's income
27 Mount Rushmore's site: Abbr.
29 Former New York governor
32 Transmits
33 "Golden Boy" dramatist
35 __ noire
36 Griever's exclamation
37 Golfer Jack
39 Twosome
42 Sister of Calliope
44 Some commercial promotions
47 Poisonous atmosphere
48 Caused to go
49 Danish city
51 Like beer
52 Unspoken
53 Actor Milo
55 Bona __
57 "Rotten" missile
58 Ewe's sound
59 San Francisco's __ Hill
60 Part of a science class

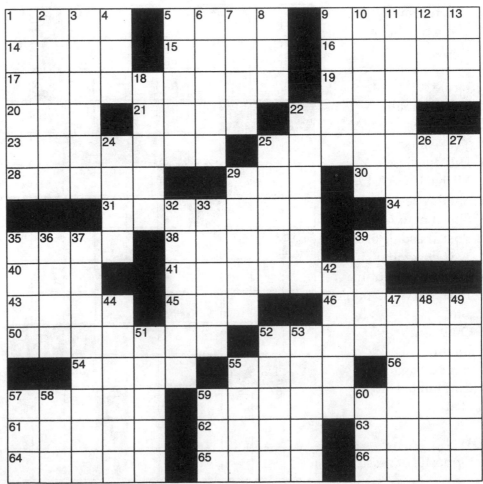

ACROSS

1 The beans in refried beans
9 Snail __ (endangered fish)
15 City south of Tijuana
16 Register
17 Battle site where the Athenians routed the Persians
18 Ford flops
19 Scene of Operation Overlord
21 Old paper currency
24 Gaffer's assistant
29 Friends' pronoun
30 Pound part
33 Druidic worship sites
34 Science shop
35 In __ (properly placed)
36 When Browning wanted to be in England
37 Montana massacre locale
41 Tired of it all
42 Some nest eggs: Abbr.
43 "Take me as __"
45 Hill dwellers
46 Michael and Peter
48 Sunday seats
49 Site of many flicks
51 Poet Teasdale et al.
52 1781 surrender site
56 Violinist Menuhin
60 1862 Maryland battle site
64 Obliterates
65 Infant
66 Heat up again
67 Candidate Harold et al.

DOWN

1 Opposite of masc.
2 Genetic inits.
3 Neighbor of Leb.
4 Dream girl in a Foster song
5 Where to put the cherry of a sundae
6 "The Wizard of Oz" actor
7 Brother of Jacob
8 Yemen's capital
9 Role in TV's "Hunter"
10 Capp and Gump
11 B.&O. et al.
12 Boot part
13 Add-on
14 "Treasure Island" monogram
20 Peacock network
21 Letters on a Cardinal's cap
22 Where Attila was defeated, 451
23 Religious experience
25 "__ the mornin'!"
26 Obstacle
27 1945 island dogfight site
28 Couturier initials
30 Heating fuel
31 Southwestern Indian
32 Ancient kingdom on the Nile
35 Criterion: Abbr.
36 Cries of delight
38 Exam
39 Like "to be": Abbr.
40 Heating fuel
41 Flock sound
44 What eds. edit
46 Oriental philosophy
47 Hafez al-Assad's land: Abbr.
48 Juries
50 Actress Winona
51 Kind of cheese
53 Okla. neighbor
54 Carpenter's fastener
55 Other: Sp.
56 "Get __ Ya-Ya's Out!" (Stones album)
57 Poet's "before"
58 Turn left
59 "Land of the free": Abbr.
61 Knot
62 Raggedy doll
63 Brit. sports cars

SIGN HERE by Gerald R. Ferguson

ACROSS

1 Quark's place
5 Some are filled out
10 Org. for 7-Down
14 Command on a submarine
15 Beethoven dedicatee
16 Get __ the ground floor
17 "Stop" sign
20 Costa del __
21 Cleanse
22 One of the Brothers Karamazov
23 "Unforgettable" singer
24 Gas or elec., e.g.
25 To pieces
28 Lustrous fabric
30 Sailor
33 Assail
34 Ted's role on "Cheers"
35 "Dies __"
36 "Stop" sign
40 Connecticut Ivy Leaguers
41 __ de la Cité
42 Marconi's invention
43 Cub's home
44 To whom Tinker threw
46 Alamogordo event
47 Bouillabaisse, e.g.
48 Table d'__
50 Chairs on poles
53 Angler's luck
54 Guy's date
57 "Stop" sign
60 German article
61 Colorful rock
62 "Pistol Packin' __"
63 Cherished
64 Wankel engine part
65 Procedure part

DOWN

1 Tacks on
2 Novice: Var.
3 Track shape
4 Kitten's cry
5 Untamed
6 Mount of __ (site near Jerusalem)
7 Astronaut Sally
8 N.Y.C. sports venue
9 When to sow
10 This meant nothing to Nero
11 Operating without __ (taking risks)
12 Skyrocket
13 "The King __"
18 Three sheets to the wind
19 Ugandan dictator
23 Game featuring shooters
24 Where Provo is
25 Invited
26 English dramatist George
27 Supped at home
29 Starwort
30 School division
31 Watering hole
32 Infatuate
35 Furious
37 Exceptional, as a restaurant or hotel
38 Went by plane
39 Gadget for cheese
44 Sicilian volcano
45 Religion of Japan
47 Not a spendthrift
49 Aquatic mammal
50 Scurried
51 Buffalo's lake
52 Actress Merrill
53 Tuckered out
54 Midge
55 Crowning point
56 "Able to __ tall buildings . . ."
58 Freudian factor
59 Early hrs.

12 NAME THAT THEME by Jeff Herrington

ACROSS

1 Sluggers' stats
5 Theme of this puzzle
10 Capital of Italia
14 Burn soother
15 Filibuster, in a way
16 Hawaiian music makers
17 Editor's definition of this puzzle's theme
20 Prevent legally
21 Popular beverage brand
22 Shea nine
25 More crafty
26 Allowable
30 Beckon
33 University of Maine site
34 __-do-well
35 Dickens protagonist
38 Mapmaker's definition of this puzzle's theme
42 Compass heading
43 Pseudonymous short-story writer
44 Backing for an exhibit
45 Peaceful
47 Sentient
48 Insurance giant
51 Negative in Nuremberg
53 Competed in the Hambletonian
56 Ribeye, e.g.
60 Physician's definition of this puzzle's theme
64 Bank claim
65 Battery part
66 Second in command
67 Driver's license prerequisite
68 The __ Prayer
69 Interested look

DOWN

1 Genre for Notorious B.I.G.
2 Depressed
3 Charged particles
4 Split-off group
5 Stylish auto
6 Man-mouse link
7 Back muscle, familiarly
8 Redding of 60's soul
9 "Open 24 hours" sign, maybe
10 Muss up
11 Animal with zebra-striped legs
12 Actress Oberon
13 Questioner
18 Indian drum
19 Political cartoonist Thomas
23 Kid's make-believe telephone
24 Elude the doorman
26 Canter
27 Ayatollah's land
28 Dunce cap, essentially
29 __ pinch
31 Where St. Mark's Cathedral is
32 Investment vehicle, for short
35 Famous tower locale
36 Roman road
37 See 49-Down
39 Enzyme suffix
40 Shanty
41 Bird's cry
45 Purpose
46 "Phooey!"
48 Not perfectly upright
49 With 37-Down, famous W.W. II correspondent
50 Big handbags
52 Wight and Man
54 List shortener
55 Singer Martin, to friends
57 Therefore
58 In awe
59 Basketball's Malone
61 Neither's companion
62 Do basic arithmetic
63 Society column word

ACROSS

1 Procter & Gamble bar
6 Native Alaskan
11 Spoil
14 Midwest airport hub
15 Sergeant at TV's Fort Baxter
16 Diamonds
17 Place to place a wallet or handkerchief
19 __ Na Na
20 Thanksgiving meat request
21 "Entry of Christ into Brussels" painter James
23 Scott Adams's put-upon comics hero
27 Nautical spar
29 Body parts shaped like punching bags
30 W.W. II Philippine battle site
31 Horse in a harness race
32 1924 Ferber novel
33 Little newt
36 It's NNW of Oklahoma City
37 Rounded lumps
38 Nicholas I or II, e.g.
39 Mule of song
40 Nash's two-l beast
41 Hardly elegant
42 Easy two-pointers
44 Concert halls
45 Starts of tourneys
47 Last course
48 Peres's predecessor
49 "__ That a Shame"
50 Eggs
51 "Come on!"
58 __ canto (singing style)
59 Characteristic
60 Confuse

61 Right-angle joint
62 Steinbeck migrants
63 Dapper

DOWN

1 __ a plea
2 "Now I see!"
3 Beatnik's exclamation
4 Skill
5 Sweetheart's assent
6 Cancel, as a launch
7 Drub
8 Lodge member
9 Luau instrument
10 Alternative to a purse
11 Err on stage
12 Cause for blessing?
13 Get ready for battle again
18 Average figures
22 Org. for Bulls and Bullets
23 Fools
24 Ex-Mrs. Trump
25 Four-time Emmy-winning comedienne
26 Ran, as colors
27 __ the Hutt, of "Star Wars"
28 Medical suffix
30 Certain mikes
32 Knee hits
34 Mountebank
35 Lovers' engagement
37 Rather morose

38 Suns
40 Deceiving
41 Nuclear treaty subject
43 "The Greatest"
44 __ cava (path to the heart)
45 Explore
46 "Boléro" composer
47 They're losing propositions
49 French friend
52 Bother
53 __ tai (drink)
54 Nutritional abbr.
55 N.Y.C. summer clock setting
56 Model Carol
57 Lock opener

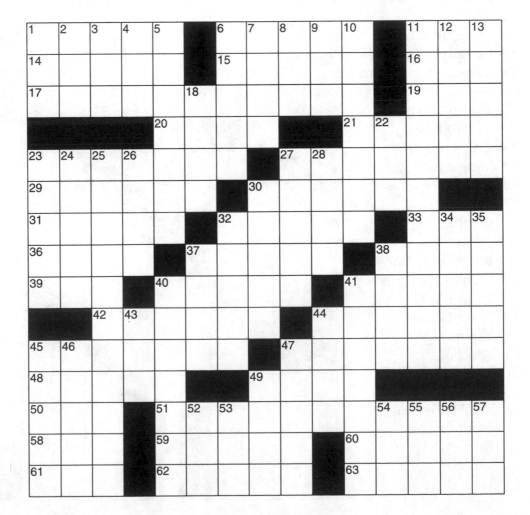

14 MATCHED SETS by Gregory E. Paul

ACROSS

1 Farm structure
5 Kon-Tiki wood
10 Boutique
14 Rev. Roberts
15 From the East
16 Windex target
17 Conjointly
19 Killer whale film
20 Till bill
21 Plant part
22 Ham
24 Certain pints
25 Vessel
26 Novelist-screenwriter Eric
29 Person in need of salvation
32 Places to buy cold cuts
33 Dugout
34 Showtime rival
35 Greatly
36 Where Joan of Arc died
37 Wilde's "The Ballad of Reading __"
38 Catty remark?
39 Vine fruit
40 Snorkeler's sight
41 "O Pioneers!" setting
43 Talkative
44 Joins the team?
45 Stable newborn
46 Insignia
48 Sheryl Crow's "__ Wanna Do"
49 Kind of story
52 Handyman Bob
53 Bobby Vinton hit
56 Word after pig or before horse
57 Burdened
58 Tittle
59 Ribald
60 Works in the cutting room
61 Midterm, e.g.

DOWN

1 Part of London or Manhattan
2 Teheran's land
3 Rural route
4 Like a centenarian
5 Back-and-forth
6 Grate expectations?
7 Actor Neeson
8 __ Diego
9 "Father Knows Best" family name
10 Lampoons
11 Sidney Sheldon TV series
12 Some time ago
13 Fruit cocktail fruit
18 Tropical getaways
23 Pal, Down Under
24 Dismounted
25 "We'll go to __, and eat bologna . . ."
26 Rhett's last words
27 Free-for-all
28 Detailed account
29 Singer Nyro or Branigan
30 German sub
31 Candy on a stick, informally
33 Parts of wine bottles
36 Look like
37 Soccer score
39 Enter a Pillsbury contest
40 Mountain range
42 Hero of early French ballads
43 Punctuation marks
45 Armada
46 Like Satan
47 Bog
48 German auto
49 Gin flavor
50 Scoreboard stat
51 Cop's milieu
54 Youth
55 Bridle part

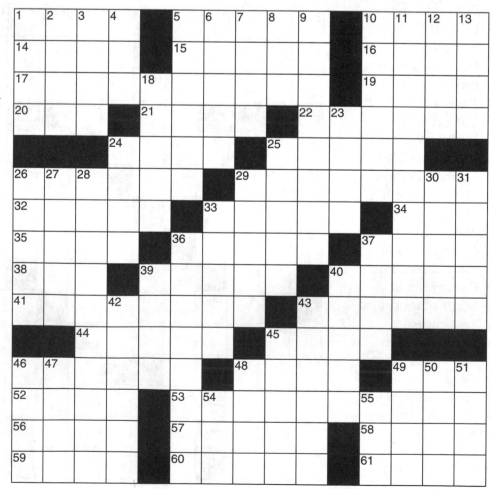

15 CHANGE OF ADDRESS by Elizabeth C. Gorski

ACROSS
1 Utters
5 Military plane acronym
10 Desertlike
14 Wyoming neighbor
15 Striped critter
16 Hurting
17 State of financial independence
19 CAT __
20 Singer Lopez
21 Kett of old comics
22 Little guitars
23 Singer Cara
25 Guard
27 It's a stitch!
29 Mint and sage
32 Stadium sounds
35 Basketball hoop site, often
39 Acorn, in 2020?
40 "Surfin' __" (Beach Boys hit)
41 Gandhi's title
42 Ryan's "Love Story" co-star
43 Russian space station
44 Puzzle
45 4:1, e.g.
46 Mubarak's predecessor
48 Recipe direction
50 Some Broadway shows
54 Overhead shot
57 Last name in spydom
59 "There ought to be __!"
61 Suggest itself (to)
63 Thrift shop stipulation
64 "The Birdcage" co-star
66 Possess

67 Whitney Houston's "All the Man That __"
68 Verve
69 Parrots
70 Chooses actors
71 E-mail command

DOWN
1 Winter bird food
2 Video arcade name
3 Arafat of the P.L.O.
4 Wallflower's characteristic
5 Much-publicized drug
6 Existed
7 Helps in dirty deeds

8 El Greco's birthplace
9 Underworld figure
10 Guarantee
11 Ice cream parlor order
12 "Dies __"
13 TV rooms
18 __ qua non
24 1991 Tony winner Daisy
26 "Take __ Train"
28 When repeated, a fish
30 Like a worn tire
31 T-bar sights
32 Jamaican exports
33 Pacific Rim region
34 Computer part
36 Joplin piece

37 24-hr. conveniences
38 Certain exams, for short
41 Prefix with physical
45 The Scriptures
47 Gets up
49 "__ Fire" (Springsteen hit)
51 Wired, so to speak
52 "The George & __ Show" (former talk show)
53 Fills up
55 Union rate
56 Chinese province
57 Joker's gibe
58 Rush job notation
60 Stimulate
62 Rip apart
65 Want __

16 WELL-STATED by Stephanie Spadaccini

ACROSS
1 27, to 3
5 Virgule
10 St. Nick accessory
14 The top
15 "Remember the __!"
16 "Ars Amatoria" poet
17 Surgical site in the Beaver State?
19 Kid's phrase of request
20 Chang's Siamese twin
21 Itch
22 Full moon color
24 Commedia dell'__
25 Rapper who co-starred in "New Jack City"
26 Le Carré character George
29 Methodology
32 Estate papers
33 Gunk
34 Champagne Tony of golf
36 __ vera
37 Middays
38 Money to tide one over
39 It's west of N.C.
40 Just
41 "What __ I do?"
42 Nielsen stats
44 Comic Charles Nelson __
45 Unpleasant task
46 Hospital unit
47 Declarer
50 Swiss river
51 "__ is me!"
54 Glitzy sign
55 Doc from the Old Line State?
58 Cartoonist Al
59 Chorus girls?

60 The first: Abbr.
61 Fashion's Klensch
62 1956 Four Lads hit "__ Much!"
63 It's just for openers

DOWN
1 Supergarb
2 "__ the rooftop . . ." (Christmas lyric)
3 Arctic Ocean sighting
4 Phone line abbr.
5 __-pants (wise guy)
6 Jessica of "Frances"
7 Right-hand person
8 __-cone
9 Decorated officers
10 Driver's license in the Gem State?
11 Russian "John"
12 Engine knock
13 Actress McClurg
18 Fishing gear
23 __ room
24 Sound system in the Keystone State?
25 Humor not for dummies
26 Quite a hit
27 Distance runner
28 Actress Massey
29 Chlorinated waters
30 1988 Olympics site
31 Inconsequential

33 Pagoda sounds
35 "Handy" man
37 Rural
41 Goddess of agriculture
43 Suffix with elephant
44 Least cooked
46 "Yippee!"
47 Suffix with utter
48 __ piccata
49 Kin of "Uh-oh!"
50 Envelope abbr.
51 Alert
52 Leave off
53 Periphery
56 "Strange Magic" rock band
57 1988 Dennis Quaid remake

ACROSS

1 Response to a pass?
5 Green-skinned pear
10 Plug of tobacco
14 Glazier's sheet
15 Master
16 __ avis
17 Italian wine region
18 Alberta national park
19 Fair
20 "Skeletons from the Closet" group
23 Prefix with second
24 Antique car
25 Get into trouble, in a way
28 Scant
30 Watch pocket
33 Food for a ladybug
34 Japanese plane of W.W. II
35 Don Juan
36 Lehár work, with "The"
39 Crackerjacks
40 Grays
41 Words to an audience
42 Philly-to-Norfolk dir.
43 __ Minor
44 Happy hour perch
45 __ Lanka
46 "That is so funny"
48 #1 song of 1973 and 1996
56 I-79 terminus
57 When to celebrate el año nuevo
58 __ Minor
59 Genuine Risk, for one
60 Squelched
61 Echelon
62 Prep exam, for short
63 Comic Arnold
64 Gets on the nerves of

DOWN

1 Flap
2 Pirate's punishment
3 Upfront money
4 Après-bain gowns
5 Composer Berg
6 Nifty, in the 50's
7 Primer girl
8 German composer Carl
9 Straighten, as a brow
10 Belief
11 Be afflicted with
12 Environs
13 Prop for Doug Henning
21 Lustful
22 Wilderness Campaign general
25 Parking garage features
26 Copycats
27 Kind of pillow
28 Euripides tragedy
29 Valentine's Day visitor
30 Page number
31 Surpass
32 Rim that holds a gem
34 Sharp turns
35 Early name of Haile Selassie
37 Suspicious quality
38 California Indian
43 Geller with paranormal powers
45 February forecast
46 Shore bird
47 "With __ in My Heart"
48 Shawn of the N.B.A.
49 They may be rolled over
50 Italy's capital
51 Small annoyance
52 "I __ man who wasn't there"
53 Figure in a Rimsky-Korsakov opera
54 Join
55 Shaggy oxen

ACROSS

1 Wingding
5 Commoner
9 Rabbit
14 "What have you been __?"
15 Hideout
16 "Home __"
17 Rabbit's title
18 1 for H, or 2 for He
19 Poet who wrote "The Sonnets to Orpheus"
20 Line from a Copland "Portrait"
23 Darrow of "King Kong"
24 Pilot's heading: Abbr.
25 Plains Indian
26 Political suffix
27 "Looky here!"
28 Hydroelectric project
31 Line from a Copland "Portrait"
37 Versifier Nash
38 Teachers' grp.
39 McDowall of "Planet of the Apes"
40 Line from a Copland "Portrait"
43 Married
44 "My mama done __ me"
45 Eggs
46 Year Justinian II regained the throne
48 Clothing size: Abbr.
49 Certain brain size
52 Subject of Copland's "Portrait"
56 "Go ahead and ask"
57 Sound system brand
58 Over
59 Kind of boom
60 Writer Bombeck
61 Site of the fabled forges of the Cyclopes
62 "Christina's World" painter
63 Navy diver
64 Close

DOWN

1 Good ole boy
2 It keeps a cook tied up
3 Rudder's locale
4 Telephone, slangily
5 Outlined
6 Potato pancake
7 "__ kleine Nachtmusic"
8 Kind of tube
9 Lash of old westerns
10 "A Town Like __" (Nevil Shute novel)
11 11th President
12 Like an octopus's defense
13 Bio word
21 Have in view
22 1982 cyberfilm
26 "Uh-huh"
27 Newsman Roger
28 Carpenter's groove
29 Como's "__ Love You So"
30 Baseball's "Say Hey Kid"
31 Hershey candy
32 Not fer
33 "If I Knew You Were Comin' __ Baked a Cake"
34 Pioneers
35 Motivated
36 Suburban New York college
41 Hankering
42 Like Mr. Spock's answers
46 French right
47 Fisherman's take-home
48 Cousin of a camel
49 Florence's __ Vecchio
50 Actress Verdugo
51 Egypt's Sadat
52 Tar hail
53 Archaeological find
54 A __ bagatelle
55 Normandy city
56 24-Across's opposite

ACROSS

1 Promise
5 Lowers, as the lights
9 Biblical queen's home
14 Peculiar: Prefix
15 Olympics event since 1900
16 Ached (for)
17 Emulated the sirens
18 "Alas!"
19 End of a Pindar poem
20 Mythological sculptor who really loved his work
22 Church niches
23 "Shake __!"
24 Round, full do
26 Court matter
29 Scott of antebellum legal fame
31 Crooked
35 Gladiator's place
37 Require
39 Vintage designation
40 "Nana" author
41 Nasal passage
42 38-Down, for example
43 German river
44 Disable
45 With glee
46 Deliver, in a way
48 Middle: Prefix
50 Slalom curve
51 Mineral suffixes
53 Emulates Xanthippe
55 Defeat
58 Athenian princess who was turned into a nightingale
63 Ouzo flavoring
64 Mother of Helen of Troy
65 Gen. Bradley
66 Arboreal animal
67 Ticked off
68 Fork prong
69 Snake, to Medusa?
70 Prepare 49-Down
71 Generations

DOWN

1 Thin strand
2 Singer Anita
3 Cabal
4 Inflexible teaching
5 Narc's collar
6 Daughter of Agamemnon and Clytemnestra
7 Office note
8 ". . . like you've __ ghost!"
9 Weapons for the Myrmidons
10 Queen of the Amazons
11 Son of Seth
12 Eliot hero
13 Lime coolers
21 "Everyone Says I Love You" actor
25 Hula hoops and such
26 Chin smoother
27 Wear away
28 Graf rival
30 Casual cotton
32 Eagle's home
33 Things to be filed
34 Classical-sounding cities in New York and Michigan
36 Youth who fell in love with his reflection
38 Another name for the Furies
41 Bob Hoskins's role in "Hook"
45 Kind of dancer
47 Pronounces
49 Some lunches
52 Divvy up
54 Slew
55 Creator of Mickey and Goofy
56 Lollapalooza
57 Frost
59 Leander's lover
60 Nabob of the Near East
61 One of Artie's exes
62 Greek war god

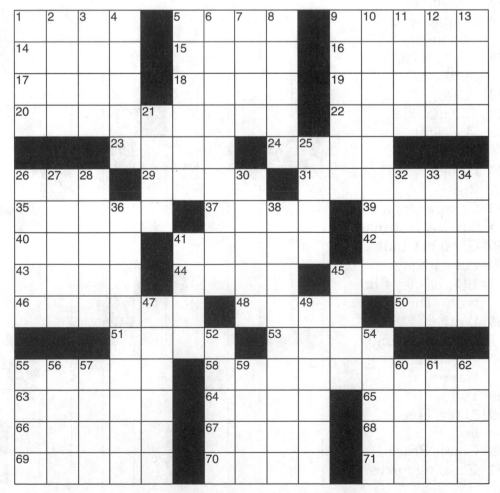

20 FANTASTIC CHARACTERS by Glenn E. Sykes

ACROSS
1 Two out of two
5 Holy war
10 Take illegally
14 Ambience
15 Writer St. Johns
16 Part of A.D.
17 Anne Morrow Lindbergh book
20 How two hearts may beat
21 Gluck and Mahler
22 Corp. honcho
23 Hill dweller
25 Furtive fellow
27 Superior
32 Actor Depardieu
35 Netanyahu's land: Abbr.
36 Cap feature
38 Double-reed instrument
39 Michael Landon portrayal
43 "Dies __"
44 Tijuana title
45 Sky sight
46 Tie up
49 Banter
51 Rigs
53 Compass point
54 Actress Thurman
56 Chou of China
59 Fill with joy
63 1941 Disney film, with "The"
66 Women, condescendingly
67 To have, in Le Havre
68 Twine
69 "Born Free" lioness
70 Comic Bruce
71 Clashing forces?

DOWN
1 Rum-soaked cake
2 Sharers' word
3 Jazz combo, often
4 Political theorist Arendt
5 Preserves
6 Bright thought
7 Get better
8 Grads
9 Vietnamese seaport
10 Anatomical pouch
11 Loaf
12 Concerning
13 Not stereo
18 John Calvin's city
19 Words of understanding
24 H.S. math
26 Lined up
27 Command to the band
28 Rhone tributary
29 Montana's second-largest city
30 Takes advantage of
31 Megalomaniac's desire
33 John who married Pocahontas
34 Moll Flanders's creator
37 Russo of "Tin Cup"
40 Radar's soft drink
41 Lariat
42 Desk item
47 Board member
48 Video store transaction
50 Tie up again
52 Drudge
54 Push
55 Ground grain
57 Auth. unknown
58 Pack __ (give up)
60 Popeyed
61 Mower maker
62 Aims
64 "Born in the __"
65 Not sweet

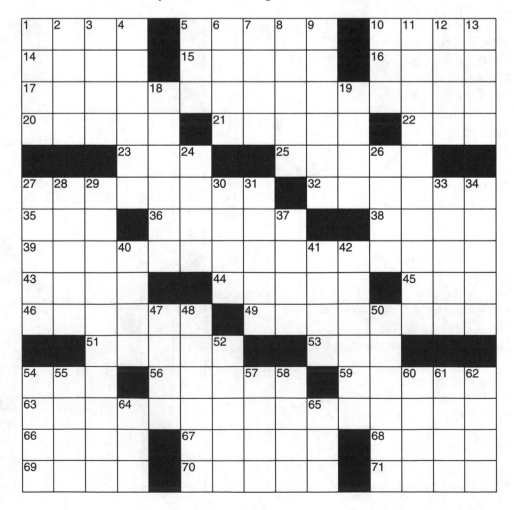

21 BOTH SIDES NOW *by Michael S. Maurer*

ACROSS

1 "Stat!"
5 Grow dim
9 Stop __
14 "__ Barry Turns 40" (1990 best seller)
15 Oak variety
16 Begot
17 Mark of Zorro?
18 Ring site
19 1954 Oscar-winning composer
20 "Anatomy of a Murder": Defense
23 Singer with the 1991 #1 hit "Rush, Rush"
26 Pupils' spots
27 "Anatomy of a Murder": Prosecution
32 Affectedly creative
33 Stadium since 1964
34 __ Club (retail chain)
38 __ du Diable
39 Because
41 Chance
42 Rebuilder of Rome
44 Plenty
45 Zhivago's love
46 "Inherit the Wind": Prosecution
50 Classic work by Montaigne
53 Extra
54 "Inherit the Wind": Defense
59 The Law of Moses
60 Ages
61 Unhinged
65 Missouri river
66 Players
67 "Whoops!"
68 Not as bright
69 MOMA artist
70 Risqué

DOWN

1 Pitches
2 Animal pouch
3 A Gardner
4 Swearing falsely
5 Medium of this puzzle's theme
6 __ vera
7 Presidential candidate who campaigned from prison
8 They've split
9 Maintain
10 Dolts
11 __ dust
12 Category
13 "Golden Boy" playwright
21 High school subj.
22 Uncle José
23 Once more
24 Tuesday night fixture on early NBC
25 Adoring one
28 Double curve
29 Tot
30 Gent from Argentina
31 Chollas
35 "__ Day's Night"
36 __ Island, Fla.
37 Hall-of-Fame pitcher Warren
40 Computer key
43 At the point in one's life
45 Word repeated in a children's rhyme
47 Higher in fuel-to-air ratio
48 Vane dir.
49 Big __
50 Prevent legally
51 Bride, in Brescia
52 Pertaining to ecological stages
55 Torture device
56 Small duck
57 A Kennedy
58 Pot starter
62 "I see!"
63 Big gobbler
64 Short

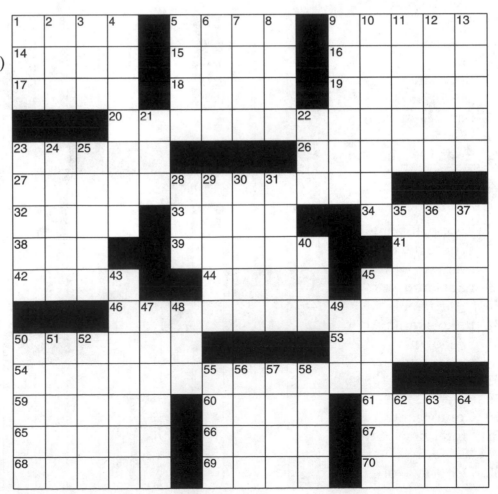

22 IN TENSE by Brendan Emmett Quigley

ACROSS

1 Cookbook phrase
4 You can't control it
9 Ramadan observance
13 Beaujolais, say
14 Rock band named for an inventor
15 Mr. T group
17 Fraternity letter
18 Hunter of myth
19 A masked man
20 Looking through photo albums, perhaps?
23 Baseball's Sandberg
24 Reactor part
25 Posed
26 Place to lose oneself
27 Emasculate
30 "Now I see!"
31 Supped
32 Like some eligibles, once
33 Eponymous physicist
35 Party item
41 Weed
42 Caps Lock neighbor, on a computer
43 Something to shoot for
44 Zeppo, for one
47 Where the buffalo roam
49 Label info
50 __ pro nobis
51 Bilko's rank: Abbr.
52 57-Down measurement
53 #1 movie of 1985
59 Singer Cara
60 Composer Copland
61 "Interview with the Vampire" co-star
62 Debussy work

63 Post-toast sound
64 "Independence Day" villains
65 High schooler
66 Some cigarettes
67 Like a wallflower

DOWN

1 Declare as fact
2 Highbrows
3 One critically examining
4 Hot spot
5 Prefix with scope or meter
6 "Q __ queen"
7 Work hard
8 Repeated word
9 Disconcerted
10 Over
11 Hoverer near God's throne
12 Human ankle
16 Words on a coat of arms
21 Suffix with Alp
22 Center of a roast
26 Queen described by Mercutio
27 Experience
28 Cultural org.
29 Central American native
30 Wake-up times: Abbr.
32 Surprised cry
34 "Just hold everything!"
36 "__ 1138" (1971 sci-fi film)

37 UPS cargo: Abbr.
38 Connoisseurs
39 Home of Mary and Joseph
40 Italian numero
44 Shell competitor
45 Genesis mount
46 Flower part
48 Go at
49 Wait
51 Unaccommodating
52 Street toughs
54 Baby-bouncing locale
55 Vigorous
56 Land of poetry
57 Printer's choice
58 Accommodating

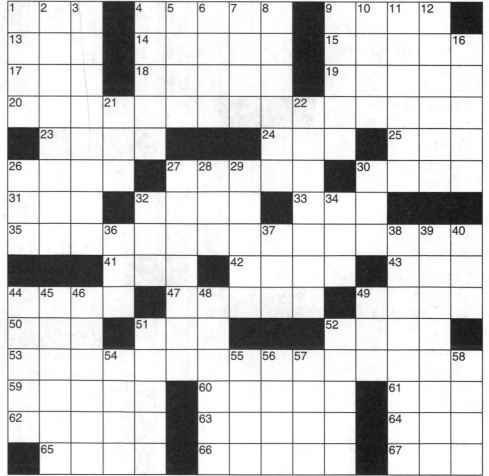

ACROSS

1 __ center
4 Protection against chills
9 Biting
14 Listening device
15 Shire of "For Richer, For Poorer"
16 Paint ingredient
17 Saddam Hussein's title
20 Playful water animal
21 "Speed" name
22 Popular N.B.A. nickname
23 They avail themselves of Vail
26 __ Canals
29 "The Joy Luck Club" author
30 A & W rival
31 Con job
32 This is one for the books
33 Dwellers along the Volga
35 Informative dialogues
38 Not moving
39 Resell at inflated prices
40 Run amok
41 Marquee names
42 %: Abbr.
45 Computer's "guts," for short
46 Bomb tryouts
48 Prefix with space or stat
49 Title for Cervantes
51 Persian Gulf nation
52 Most typewriters have them
57 Spine-tingling
58 Freeze
59 "Hold On Tight" rock group

60 Office furniture
61 Part of a spool
62 "__ Misérables"

DOWN

1 Send another E-mail message
2 Actress Kitt
3 Canea resident
4 Move a muscle
5 "It __ to Be You"
6 Pintful, perhaps
7 Take the gold
8 Potato pancakes
9 Code words for "A"
10 He went east of Eden
11 Ancient Italian
12 Stephen of "The Crying Game"

13 Diagonal chess capture
18 Et __ (and the following)
19 "The Star-Spangled Banner" preposition
23 1978 Peace Prize winner
24 Actor Kristofferson
25 Mensa hurdles
27 Galley items
28 Meditation syllables
30 Signs of winter's end
31 Word in an octagon
32 Work without __ (risk injury)
33 Some Romanovs
34 Suffers
35 Common swab

36 Firebrands
37 Imitate Mel Tormé
38 Pinball path
41 Pianist Rudolf
42 "Stormy" sea bird
43 Hold protectively
44 Some sculptures
46 Poker payments
47 Slinky or yo-yo
48 Motel approver, briefly
50 Estrada of "CHiPs"
51 Hebrew letter before resh
52 Proof finale
53 Minuscule
54 "The Island of the Day Before" author
55 To date
56 Tampa Bay player, for short

24 NAME GAME by Richard Silvestri

ACROSS

1 Bar fare
6 "Merry old" king of rhyme
10 Drivel
13 Shiraz native
14 Moundsman Hershiser
15 Make a pitch
16 Trattoria staple
17 Noodges
18 Atahualpa was one
19 Where an actress can see forever?
22 "Gunsmoke" appeared on it
25 Original sinner
26 Kickoff aid
27 Suffix with labyrinth
28 Black-and-white snack
30 Golden Fleece craft
32 Horse opera
34 Jamboree locale
36 Hwy.
37 Obese author's admission?
42 E.R. devices
43 More exquisite
44 Lawn game
47 Terrarium plant
48 China setting
49 A "Road" destination
50 Columbus initials
52 Candle count
54 Strive
55 Masochistic trumpeter's prediction?
59 Fine-edged
60 Peek-__
61 Disconcerted
65 Messes up

66 Oversupply
67 Hopping mad
68 Compass pt.
69 Antitoxins
70 Himalayan kingdom

DOWN

1 Sample, as wine
2 Coach Parseghian
3 Vegas opening
4 Opposed
5 "Cheers" character
6 Orchestral offering
7 Spoken
8 Smoothly, to Solti
9 Old comic actress __ Janis
10 Learned one
11 Secret
12 Cast member
15 Get a move on
20 Profits
21 Go back into business
22 Caesar's sidekick
23 Source of fiber
24 Highway hauler
29 Kind of nerve
31 Crystal-lined rock
33 Dog from Japan
35 Delivery person?
36 Emotional pang

38 Circus Hall of Fame site
39 Main point
40 One who succeeds
41 Busboy's pickup
44 Part of a road test
45 Edmonton icemen
46 Stick together
47 Gridiron mishap
51 Bucks
53 Puckish
56 Election winners
57 Part of B.Y.O.B.
58 Make out
62 Skip, as commercials
63 Hellenic vowel
64 Singer Shannon

(25) MEET THE FLINTSTONES by Mark Elliot Skolsky

ACROSS

1 Abnormal vesicle
5 Longtime Boston Symphony conductor
10 D.E.A. officer
14 Miles per hour, e.g.
15 Suburban San Francisco county
16 Like an octopus's defense
17 Inter __
18 Parenthetical comment
19 Saintly
20 The Flintstones' favorite track star?
23 "__ pray"
24 NASA launch concern
28 Carl Reiner's "Where's __?"
32 Daunt
33 Drink from a dish
36 The Flintstones' favorite dancer?
39 Greek concert sites
41 Steal away
42 Cattle encourager
43 The Flintstones' favorite Congressman?
46 Calendar spans: Abbr.
47 Drain
48 Popular Deco lithographs
50 Covets
53 Organize, as an exhibit
57 The Flintstones' favorite baker?
61 Skater Starbuck
64 Bunk
65 Word in many Gardner titles
66 "The Art of Love" poet

67 Fish
68 "Cómo __ usted?"
69 Pebbles, e.g., on "The Flintstones"
70 Actress Patricia et al.
71 Day of __

DOWN

1 Swimming stroke
2 Bulldog
3 Circus prop
4 Join forces (with)
5 Bradley or Sharif
6 Pitts of "Life with Father"
7 Droughtlike
8 Golf __
9 Give extreme unction to, old-style
10 Brandy, perhaps
11 Year in Spain
12 "Citizen Kane" studio
13 Dancer Charisse
21 Beginning
22 History
25 Dangerous, colloquially
26 Trial's partner
27 Oboes, e.g.
29 Quarry
30 Ill-gotten gains
31 Put on a pedestal
33 Like oak leaves
34 "There Is Nothin' Like __"
35 Police blotter types
37 Be on __ with (equal)

38 Posted
40 Immunity unit
44 Australia's largest lake
45 __ Sabe
49 Football
51 Wharton's "__ Frome"
52 Best Director of 1986 and 1989
54 Imperial decree
55 Settles in
56 Doctor
58 Hatha-__
59 Word with T or dry
60 Whiskeys
61 Psalms preceder
62 Fertility clinic needs
63 Foresail

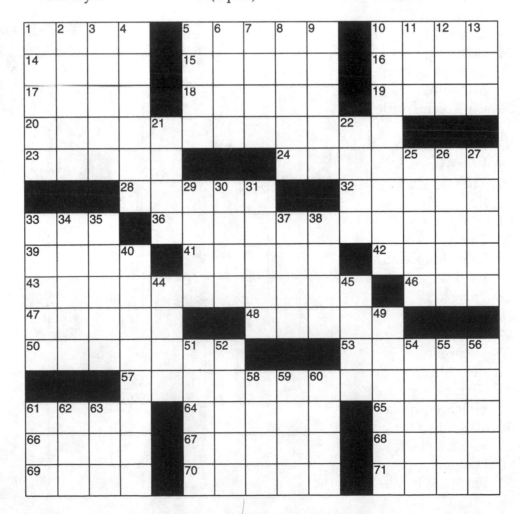

DOG TAILS by Norman S. Wizer

ACROSS

1 Cheek
5 Runs in neutral
10 Latitude
14 Woody's son
15 State capital or its river
16 Artist Magritte
17 Ham operator's dog?
19 Prefix with -hedron
20 Napkin's place
21 Buffalo hunter
22 Feast of Lots honoree
24 Dam
25 Showing a fancy for
26 Cooked cereal
29 Kind of roll
33 Think a thought
34 Reading, for a famous example
35 Mishmash
36 Called the butler
37 Not set
38 Large green moth
39 Work units
40 They're kept under lids at night
41 __ the hills
42 Drop in
44 Least laugh-out-loud, as humor
45 Parroted
46 Can't stand
47 Two-dimensional
50 Future jr.
51 Leg. title
54 Kharagpur queen
55 Hairdresser's dog?
58 30's migrant
59 Flip chart site
60 Woolen caps
61 Farmer's locale?
62 Metric unit
63 Boxer's stat

DOWN

1 Satirist Mort
2 Gazetteer info
3 Big shot in ice hockey
4 Lay turf
5 Locale of the Cantabrian Mountains
6 Mother hen, e.g.
7 Low-cal
8 Lubbock-to-Fort Worth dir.
9 In a calm manner
10 Diplomat's dog?
11 Poland's Walesa
12 Kitty feed
13 Junior, e.g.
18 Scape
23 Peter and Paul: Abbr.
24 Pilot's dog?
25 Best Actor of 1990
26 Shouts on the links
27 Disjointedly
28 Spoken-word #1 hit of 1964
29 One administering corporal punishment
30 Shake off
31 Hirschfeld hidings
32 Brown
34 Reinforced with a rope
37 Exhibits dyslexia
41 Lawn products brand
43 W.W. II agcy.
44 Parti-colored
46 Noted marine watercolorist
47 Egg on
48 Cottage site
49 Indigo dye
50 Enclosure with a MS
51 Neighbor of Minn.
52 Pollster Roper
53 Hero of 60's TV and 80's film
56 Toque, for one
57 Six-time home run champ

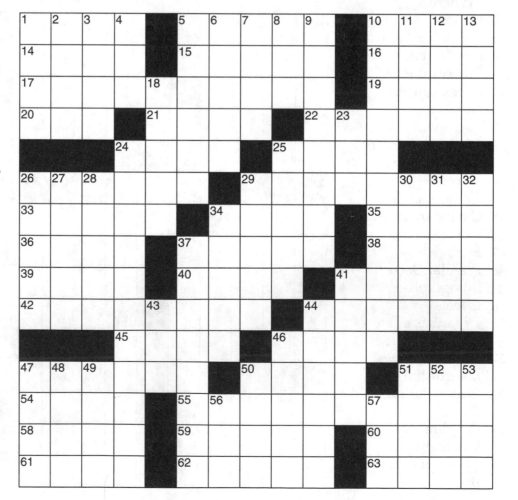

ACROSS

1 Screamer's necessity
6 Manhandle
9 "Peer Gynt" dramatist
14 "Otello," e.g.
15 __ mode
16 It makes quite a bang
17 Sound of old floorboards
18 When Guy Fawkes Day is celebrated: Abbr.
19 It may be static
20 Cult Canadian comedy troupe, with "The"
23 Operates
24 Tara family
25 Flood stage
28 __ Xing (sign)
29 "The Gold Bug" author
30 Need air conditioning
32 60's war capital
34 Boy or girl lead-in
35 1869 Twain book, with "The"
41 Season of peace
42 Move stealthily
43 Provided for, as a widow
47 N.Y.C. clock setting
48 Liq. measures
51 Gives the green light
52 Of service
54 Untouched
55 1934 Lillian Hellman play, with "The"
58 Genius
60 Hood's gun
61 Item on a pole
62 Plane seating choice

63 Charlottesville sch.
64 And __ grow on
65 Gibson, e.g.
66 Gibson, e.g.
67 Victim of a 1955 coup

DOWN

1 Poky
2 Revolt
3 Had to have
4 Not Astroturf
5 H.H. Munro, pseudonymically
6 Roman temple
7 56-Down salutation
8 Isn't decisive
9 If

10 Unwelcome mail
11 Heel style
12 Sea bird
13 Yule serving
21 Peter of Herman's Hermits
22 Hem's partner
26 Home video format
27 Carpenter's nail
29 Campaign money source
31 Harmless prank
32 Reason for darning
33 "__ De-Lovely"
35 Prefix with Chinese
36 Cranny's partner

37 10:00 program
38 Bony
39 "Homage to Clio" poet
40 Diner sandwich
44 Spoiler
45 Immigrant's study, for short
46 Cotton-pickin'
48 Citer
49 Loyally following
50 Address of St. Patrick's Cathedral?
53 Plucky
54 Drop a dime, so to speak
56 See 7-Down
57 Call it a day
58 Farm call
59 Rock's Ocasek

ACROSS

1 Jim at the bar
5 Long Island town
10 "Want to hear a secret?"
14 It's tender in Turin
15 Actress Gia
16 Bar assoc. member
17 Like a gemologist's drinks?
19 Kisser
20 Migrants' advocate Chavez
21 Sans mixers
22 Latest thing
23 Carafe quantity
25 Fictional hotel hellion
27 First-rate
30 Static __
31 Film director Wertmuller
32 Adventure hero __ Williams
35 Grateful?
38 Tailward, on jets
39 Sangria container
41 Gentle handling, initially
42 __ dicit (legal refusal)
44 Ike's onetime singing partner
45 Luau entertainment
46 Skip over
48 Worker with a scythe
50 "The Song of the Earth" composer
52 Highly hackneyed
54 Baseball's Jesus
55 Actor Guinness
57 Gin flavorers
61 Asset
62 Like a platform diver's drinks?
64 Mislay

65 Fur source
66 Sparkling wine spot
67 Baa-maids?
68 In the poorhouse
69 Two semesters

DOWN

1 Voting group
2 Deutsche article
3 Song and dance, e.g.
4 Gospel's Jackson
5 Mt. Carmel site: Abbr.
6 Treat with tea
7 One who spikes the punch
8 Chase of "Now, Voyager"
9 Drawing that's easy on the eyes
10 Bar regulars, e.g.
11 Like an astronaut's drinks?
12 Deer sirs
13 Melville adventure
18 Lexicographer Partridge
24 TV's Hatcher
26 Detector target
27 Scotch family
28 LP player
29 Like a roofer's drinks?
30 Lawyer Roy
33 Diminutive suffix
34 Sprint rival
36 Word for a madame
37 Lasting impression
39 Barre room bend
40 Bring home
43 Mistreats
45 Vestibule
47 Tap
49 Part of SEATO
50 Fudge flavor
51 Let have
52 Davis of "Now, Voyager"
53 Hurt
56 Miller beer option
58 Seine feeder
59 "Cómo __ usted?"
60 Do a bartending job
63 It may finish second

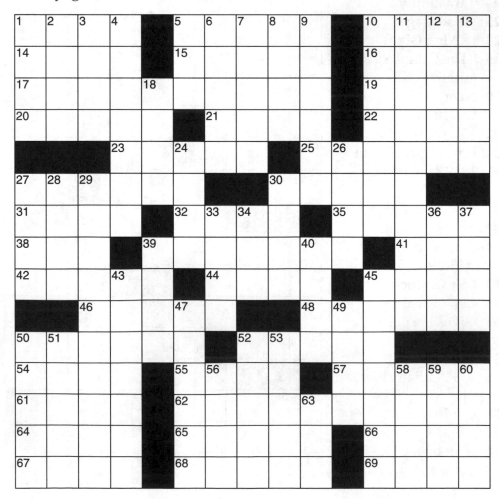

ACROSS

1 Made fun of
6 Comic Martin
11 Object of invective, often
14 Concert venue
15 Site of Western Michigan University
17 1959 Philip Roth book
19 Part of the Holy Trinity
20 First name on Capitol Hill, once
21 Cold war side, with "the"
22 Seats with cushions
23 1932 and 1981 "Tarzan" films, e.g.
26 Inevitably
29 Dove rival
30 Coin no longer minted
31 Gen. Powell
32 Charge
35 Hemingway novel of 1929
39 Dem. opponent
40 Watergate co-conspirator
41 Nonsense word repeated in a 1961 hit
42 Chemistry measurements
43 1902 Physics Nobelist Pieter
45 Loudly laments
48 Add color to
49 Seat
50 The "pneumo" in pneumonia
51 Untapped
54 1958 Mario Lanza song
59 Popular motor home
60 Writer Shute
61 Article in France Soir
62 Give
63 Ennoble

DOWN

1 Certain sports cars, informally
2 Suffix with buck
3 Drudge
4 Get rid of
5 Actor Coleman
6 Biases
7 Mediator's skill
8 "Hold On Tight" rock band
9 Kilmer of "The Saint"
10 Aussie bird
11 Language spoken in Tashkent
12 Cursor mover
13 Puts up, as a computer message
16 Home products company
18 Evergreens
22 Jack of 50's-60's TV
23 Come-from-behind attempt
24 Send out
25 Jorge's hand
26 Winglike
27 Never-ending sentence?
28 Scarf
29 Causes of some absences
31 Turns over
32 Gift tag word
33 Austen heroine
34 Cable staple
36 "The Time Machine" race
37 Something left behind
38 Help
42 Cheech of Cheech and Chong
43 Vitamin additive
44 Head of a train
45 More than a scuffle
46 Chill-inducing
47 Alerts
48 "Presumed Innocent" author
50 Lincoln Log competitor
51 Astronomer's sighting
52 Disney's "__ and the Detectives"
53 Cartoonist Kelly
55 Churchill symbol
56 Surveyor's dir.
57 Pop
58 Latin ruler

ACROSS

1 How the boss wants things done, briefly
5 Ditto
9 Devil dolls, e.g.
14 Kind of chop
15 "Family Ties" kid
16 Dander
17 "Oh, woe!"
18 Chimney covering
19 Nick name?
20 "Don't tell!"
23 "Losing My Religion" rock group
24 Scene of the William Tell legend
25 Norma Webster's middle name
26 Cash substitute
27 Certain corporate career path
33 Beam
34 Carthage founder
35 Julia, on "Seinfeld"
38 "__ Three Lives"
40 Reggae relative
42 Brit. decorations
43 New York county
46 Reaching as far as
49 Easter parade attraction
50 1948 Irene Dunne film
53 Foldaway, e.g.
55 Polit. designation
56 Maiden name preceder
57 __ Arbor
58 Western mountain range
64 Shade tree
66 Equine shade
67 "Let's Make a Deal" choice

68 "Victory __" (1954 film)
69 Secular
70 Designer Cassini
71 Forfeits
72 Swirl
73 "And away __!"

DOWN

1 In __ (having trouble)
2 George Takei TV/film role
3 Sixth-day creation
4 "Playing" critter
5 Japanese fish dish
6 Facial tissues additive
7 Doorsill cry
8 Obtain by force
9 Poker boo-boo
10 Mouths, anatomically
11 Eastern taxi: Var.
12 Prefix with arthritis
13 Sea World attraction
21 Walked (on)
22 Scarce
27 Chamber group, maybe
28 Dutch painter
29 See firsthand
30 Clinic workers, for short
31 Mammy __
32 Lowlife
36 Linguist Chomsky
37 "Cómo __ usted?"

39 German article
41 Police radio msg.
44 Japanese entertainers
45 Old Dodge
47 Period of a renter's agreement
48 Provo neighbor
51 Channel swimmer Gertrude
52 Grazing area
53 Plot
54 "You're __ talk!"
59 Way to go
60 Bust, so to speak
61 Handout
62 Film director Nicolas
63 "Cogito __ sum"
65 Middling mark

31 PYRAMID SCHEME by Norman S. Wizer

ACROSS
1 Serve with a summons
5 "Casino" co-star, 1995
10 Castaway's transportation
14 Copper containers
15 Hybrid citrus fruit
16 Perry's creator
17 Egyptian actress?
19 Jar
20 Ar's follower
21 Novelist Jean
22 Come to
24 Last frame, sometimes
26 Chorus syllables
28 Winter resort rentals
30 Like some drugs
33 It may be hooked
36 Philippic
38 Navigator's dir.
39 Garfield's predecessor
41 Setting for a place setting
42 Room to __
44 "Gotcha!"
45 Guesses
48 __ out (manages)
49 Pleasing to the ear
51 Bridge
53 Waste gases, e.g.
55 Storm
59 Fivesome
61 Twelve Oaks neighbor
63 Trifle
64 House of Leo?
65 Egyptian heavyweight?
68 1995 N.C.A.A. basketball champs
69 Overact

70 Personal prefix
71 "__ My Girl" (1967 hit)
72 Fabulous
73 Get dewy-eyed

DOWN
1 Hale-Bopp, e.g.
2 People with "O'" names
3 Flirt
4 Paranormal ability
5 Strong praise
6 Where 2-Down live
7 Baby-size
8 Murmur
9 Went all the way, as a smoker

10 Used car deal, e.g.
11 Egyptian second banana?
12 Kind of pipe
13 Ky.-Ala. divider
18 Amount of hair
23 Evanesces
25 Salinger dedicatee
27 Playing marbles
29 "My love is like a red, red rose," e.g.
31 Apropos of
32 Medium grades
33 "Eh?"
34 Island near Kauai
35 Egyptian actor?
37 Commanded
40 Bulgaria's capital

43 Pocket protector items
46 Splash sites
47 Thinner
50 They're cast in a cast of thousands
52 "Immediately!"
54 Sitting place
56 Offhand remark
57 Ancient land on the Aegean
58 Egypt's Temple of __
59 In addition
60 Individually
62 You have to be upfront about this
66 Big bird
67 Top 10 song, say

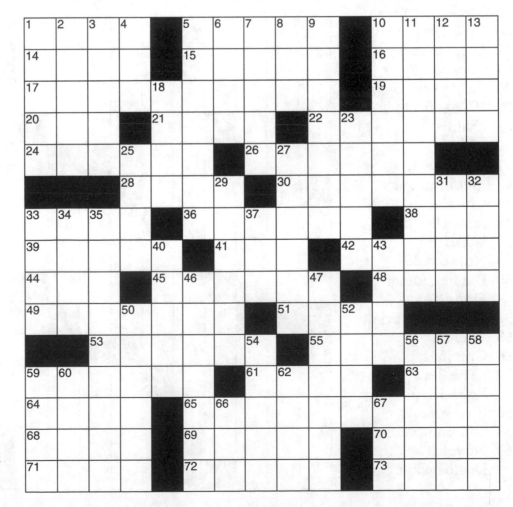

ACROSS

1 Bouquet holder
5 Bouquet makers
10 __ Offensive
13 Deejay Don
14 Two-time Grand Slam winner
15 Missile housing
16 "Relax!"
19 __ gratia artis
20 "I have half __ to . . ."
21 Part of a bouquet
22 The Beatles' last movie
24 Brush, so to speak
25 Baseball's Charlie Hustle
26 Meager
28 Monopoly token
30 Mall component
31 Legal matter
34 "Relax!"
38 Be in hock
39 1977 U.S. Open champ
40 Likable
41 Manipulate
42 Predominant
44 Chiseler
46 James Bond backdrop
49 Not so bold
50 Former Soviet First Lady
52 Guinness specialty
53 "Relax!"
56 Cravings
57 "The Brady Bunch" housekeeper
58 Flying eagle, e.g.
59 Old polit. cause
60 Novelist Dostoevsky: Var.

61 Trojan ally, in the "Iliad"

DOWN

1 "Myra Breckinridge" author
2 That's a subject for Dean Martin!
3 Summer ailment
4 Therapy fad
5 Like a plum pudding
6 "C'est __"
7 Kenmore product
8 Crack the books
9 Semicircle
10 Indonesian island
11 Cousin of a gazelle

12 June award
15 Work like a slave
17 Items at a lost-and-found
18 First game
23 With 49-Down, "Say Anything" co-star
24 Cutting remark
26 Lieu
27 True-crime TV series
28 Simpson's criminal-case judge
29 Vulgar
30 Peddle
31 It's found in a runoff
32 And so on

33 1967 Monkees song
35 Zoo section
36 Dr. Atkins's plan
37 Oklahoma town
41 Blubbers
42 Participant at a 90's dance club
43 Jai __
44 Root on
45 One raising a howl?
46 Pancho's amigo
47 Going stag
48 Signs a lease
49 See 23-Down
50 Preside over
51 Bone-dry
54 Clod
55 Admiral competitor, once

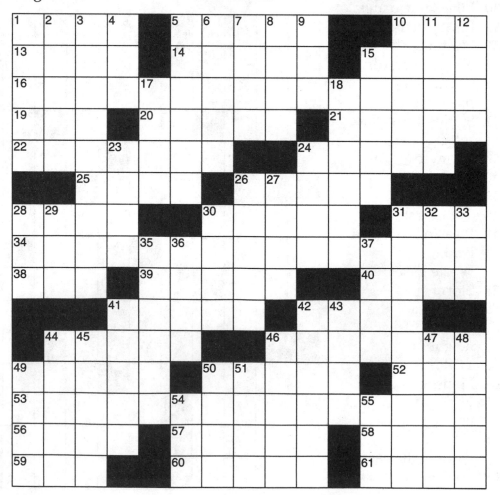

A PUZZLEMENT by David J. Kahn

ACROSS

1 Wee bit
4 Sticking point
8 Ethanol, to dimethyl ether
14 Longtime Frazier foe
15 Flunky
16 Actor William of "Knots Landing"
17 Sunday reading
19 Wilderness home
20 Explosives and such
21 "The Raggedy Man" poet
23 Frostiness
24 Latitude
25 __ Verde National Park
26 "Bird on __" (Gibson film)
28 Together, musically
29 Upbeat, in music
31 The yoke's on them
32 Patrick Ewing, for one
34 Quechua, e.g.
36 Musical that premiered 3/29/51
39 "The Faerie Queene" character
40 Thatched
43 A.L. player
46 Smack
48 Coty of France
49 Places for hats?
51 Fraternity letters
52 Lot
53 Kind of card
54 Golden Horde member
56 Mint __
57 Beer, sometimes
59 Pacific divider
61 Popular Hershey bar
62 Repute
63 B.&O. stop
64 Furtive
65 TV Guide span
66 Guitarist Nugent

DOWN

1 Southeast Florida city
2 Pie preference
3 Gymnast's finale
4 Airport queue
5 Bravo, e.g.
6 Any one of the Magi
7 Song from 36-Across
8 Nothing doing?
9 "Bye!"
10 Fertilization sites
11 60's-70's TV sleuth
12 Uncut
13 End a shutdown
18 With 27-Down, song from 36-Across
22 Psychiatrist/author R.D. __
25 Sell
27 See 18-Down
30 States of alarm
33 Suffix with slogan
35 Actress Sue __ Langdon
37 Not suitable
38 VISTA worker, perhaps
41 Understanding
42 Pool area
43 Footprints
44 __ reason
45 Con
47 Pep talk, sometimes
50 Châteaubriand
55 Pretentious
56 Weightlifting maneuver
58 Reggae variation
60 Part of Italy

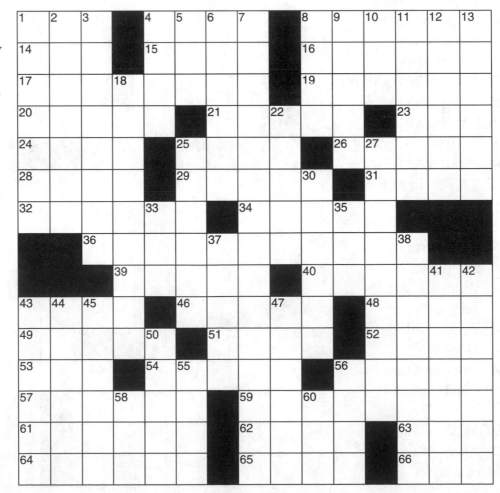

ACROSS

1 Raises
7 Coal-mining waste
11 Interruption
14 Cores
15 Grand Prix, for instance
17 One of the lanthanides
18 Accumulates
19 What's NEW?
21 Hugs, symbolically
22 Spanish dramatist __ de Vega
23 What's KNEW?
30 Fragrant resin
31 Member of the flock
32 Spill the beans
36 What's GNU?
40 Opposite of bless
41 River to the Mississippi
42 Provincial pronoun
43 What's NU?
46 Athens's home
49 Suffix with libel
50 What's NOUS?
56 "A Raisin in the Sun" writer Hansberry
57 Quiver contents
60 Support
61 Where to get fast service?
62 Derek and Diddley
63 Honky-__
64 Ancient Qumran inhabitant

2 Curse the day
3 Brown shade
4 Illegal block
5 German
6 Violent Saharan wind
7 Pane's place
8 Pear-shaped instrument
9 Fermi's fascination
10 How horror scenes are often depicted
11 Refuel
12 Intense
13 "__ Le Moko" (1937 Duvivier drama)

16 Slots site
20 Water tester
23 Intellect
24 __ Romeo
25 Skin: Suffix
26 "__ love!"
27 Gettysburg victor
28 Have the rights to
29 No longer active: Abbr.
32 Stain
33 Ill-mannered one
34 Basilica section
35 Cold one
37 Opposite of dep.
38 Obit word
39 Trash bins, graffiti, etc.

43 Track speedster
44 Chinese diplomat Wellington __
45 Crescent-shaped
46 Down East college town
47 Zebra groups
48 Pertaining to
50 Bungle
51 Seat of Hawaii County
52 Nabokov novel
53 Stench
54 Tomb items
55 Not a lick
58 Carry the day
59 Wind dir.

DOWN

1 Abbr. at the bottom of a letter

TERSE COMMENT *by David J. Kahn*

ACROSS

1 Airplane exit
5 Boat with a V-shaped transom
9 China-Russia boundary river
13 Finito
14 ". . . partridge in __ tree"
16 15th-century maritime name
17 Tuscany ta-ta
18 Choice for a sand trap shot
19 "Even __ speak . . ."
20 Start of a Will Rogers quip
23 Kind of parking
24 Miss America, to some
25 More of the quip
30 Sorrows
33 Algerian port
34 Sentimental stuff
35 Tax plan staples
36 Mallard-sized goose
37 San __, Italy
38 Horse color
39 Craving
40 Considered, with "on"
41 More of the quip
45 Unencumbered
46 Writer Jong et al.
50 End of the quip
54 Jeer
55 Kind of seal
56 View from Sandusky
57 Pond swimmer
58 Tee off
59 Insect nests
60 Muffs

61 Filmmaker Joel or Ethan
62 Something to do

DOWN

1 "Fidelio" jailer
2 Birdlike
3 Board
4 Is a breadwinner
5 Occurred to, with "on"
6 Noted cartel
7 Go back to square one on
8 __ Sant'Gria (wine brand)
9 Wreath for the head
10 Doesn't estimate correctly
11 Like some guests
12 Actress __ Dawn Chong
15 Counting (on)
21 Malady suffix
22 Charley Weaver's Mt. __
26 Like some baseball games
27 Early Warhol film
28 À votre __
29 Tough guy
30 Opera set near the Nile
31 Like Grape-Nuts vis-à-vis other cereals
32 Mustache style
36 Intermingled
37 Basic skill
40 Swamplike
42 Skis with high-speed turns
43 "Bali __"
44 Make vapid
47 Senate house in ancient Rome
48 Litmus reddeners
49 Valentino role
51 Police decoy, sometimes
52 Rock music's Police, e.g.
53 Golfer Ballesteros
54 Mobilnet corp.

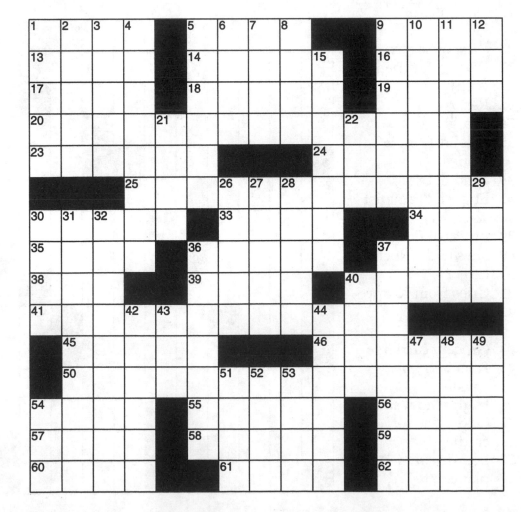

ACROSS

1 Coarse tobacco
5 Arm, to Armand
9 It holds the mayo
12 Winner of a 1944 Pulitzer
13 "Lovely __" (1967 song)
14 Garage jobs
16 Message at the dawn of Creation?
18 Daughter of Juan Carlos
19 Have coming
20 Number corresponding to an exponent
22 Milne baby
23 Patient's program
24 They're nuts
27 Daughter of Homer
28 Wife of Saturn
31 Find __ for (pair with)
32 Reserved
34 Shady way
35 "Heimskringla" stories
36 Kind of bread
37 English dramatist Thomas
39 Butler of fiction
40 He's had a Rocky career
41 Cries from Krupp
42 Produce hippie attire
43 Grocery carriers
45 Hackberry's cousin
46 High school subject
48 Odd place for a cradle
52 Board with a planchette
53 Overhears Satan tempt?
55 Words after "whether"
56 Ill temper
57 Spy in 1994 headlines
58 Shaq's alma mater
59 Copycat
60 Fast time

DOWN

1 Common tater
2 Ballyhoo
3 Start of Hamlet's "Yorick" speech
4 Produced
5 Menudo's kudos
6 Heckle
7 One-time connector
8 Helper of parable
9 Child who's six-foot-two
10 Fit for Eden?
11 Seat of Washoe County
14 "__ Weapon"
15 Droop
17 Go on and on
21 Puts one within another
24 Chiromancers read them
25 Internet messages
26 Forbidden tree décor?
27 Trademarked items
29 Glazier's goop
30 Outpouring
32 Solomon's mother
33 Fleeting
35 Factions
38 Cow catcher
39 Upset
42 Less verbose
44 Winter pear
46 __ Canals
47 Use a reverse stitch
48 Prefix with conference or commute
49 Volume
50 Receptive
51 "Hey, you!"
54 Big shot

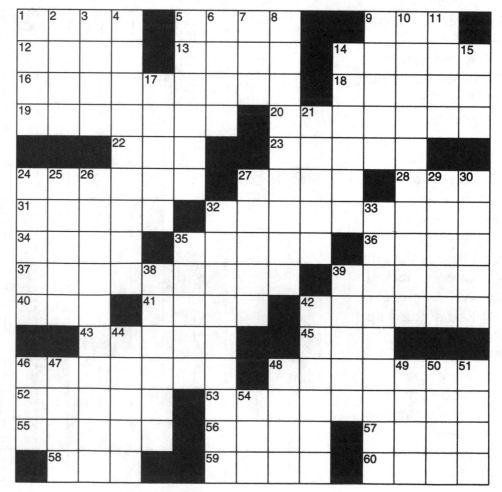

ACROSS

1 Pickle
5 Klinger portrayer, in 70's-80's TV
9 Tubby
14 Chief Whitehorse, for one
15 Cousin of a clarinet
16 Winning
17 "Yeah, right!"
18 First name in country
19 Explorer Amundsen
20 High points
23 Places for aces?
24 Operculum
25 Opposite of post-
28 Stone smoother
29 Mr. Jaggers's ward, in Dickens
30 Brat's Christmas present
31 Largest moon of Neptune
33 Sounds of a leak
34 Burdensome possession
37 Pandemonium
38 Hologram producers
39 Cold war capital
40 Price word
41 Stand for a portrait
44 Down
45 Actress Tyler of 90's films
46 Small quantity symbol, in math
48 Extremely exasperated
51 Flabbergast
53 It's next to Mayfair, in London

54 Signs
55 Director known for spaghetti westerns
56 It's all the same to moi
57 Cut, maybe
58 Joined together
59 "It just isn't __"
60 Employees' ID's: Abbr.

DOWN

1 Swine
2 The "se" in per se
3 "Beats me!"
4 Shield's purpose
5 Ontario city just west of Buffalo
6 Gives a yegg a hand
7 Biblical attire
8 Army's back section
9 Unit of capacitance
10 Sailor's salutation
11 Recipe measure
12 Baseball's Bando
13 Anomalous
21 Turns inside out
22 Dance maneuver
26 Enthralled
27 City rattlers
29 Like 19-Across's expeditions
30 Ranks
32 Broadcast

33 Musical passage
34 Horse's halter
35 Manual
36 Door feature
37 Safer workplace?
40 Pizzeria order
42 Twisty-horned animals
43 Ensure
45 Drew in
46 Actor Hawke
47 Branch headquarters?
49 Like Silver's rider
50 Inoperative
51 It's at the end of the line
52 King's name

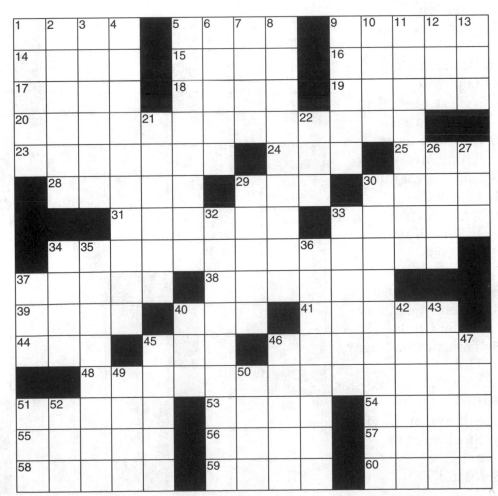

ACROSS

1 1979 exile
5 Double or triple, possibly
9 "Cantar de Rodrigo" hero
14 Actress Hatcher
15 Plod (through)
16 Nero's instrument
17 Neighbor of Albion
18 Kazakh-Uzbek sea
19 "Ghosts" writer
20 1983 Eddie Murphy movie
23 Like some letters
24 Opposite of idles
27 Run into
30 Kitchen needs
31 "Would __?" (sleazeball's question)
32 Procter & Gamble brand
33 Penultimate fairy-tale word
34 Where 61-Across was "drawn"
35 Clock settings
36 Thing, in law
37 F.D.R. program
39 "How dry __"
40 "Ah, But Your Land Is Beautiful" novelist
42 Wax
43 Flamenco cheer
44 Foreign Secretary under Churchill
45 Transport to Sugar Hill
47 Mary's "Ink" co-star
48 Brave
49 Funnyman David
51 Stock market activity
56 "Chill"
58 Not very bright
59 Hirt hit
60 Sultan Qabus bin Said, e.g.
61 The __-Neisse Line
62 Holly genus
63 Vegas casino, with "The"
64 June honorees
65 Kudzu, for one

DOWN

1 Let it stand
2 Title for Mozart
3 Horne solo
4 Caste member
5 Graceful descent
6 Chess and Risk
7 Electrical device
8 Manhattan Project physicist
9 "Beowulf," for one
10 Oldest republic in Africa
11 Big Mama
12 Bruckner's Symphony No. 7 __
13 Mafia boss
21 Detain during wartime
22 Clio winners
25 Sports commentator Dick
26 Like old nylons
27 Cut the mustard?
28 Loser of 1588
29 Overall guide
34 What a bore!
37 Had a dispute
38 Expert advice
41 Kind of road
42 Island discovered by Columbus
45 Disney acquisition of 1995
46 This will help you shoot straight
50 Indira's son
52 W.W. II side
53 Buñuel collaborator
54 Neck and neck
55 Old German duchy name
56 Bacillus shape
57 Big bird

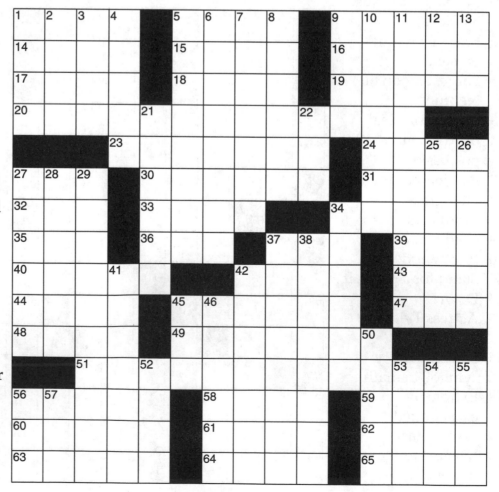

(39) BE FLEXIBLE by A.J. Santora

ACROSS
1 Santa __
5 School subj.
9 McEntire et al.
14 He follows the news
15 Perry creator
16 La Scala cheer
17 Jewish month
18 Kind of companion
19 Minipicture, maybe
20 Gawks
23 Six-foot Australian
24 Brilliance
25 Double curve
26 Uphill conveyance
27 Get it
28 Jumping-off place?
31 Squire
32 Sylvester's co-star in "Rocky"
33 Per __
38 Expense
39 About-face
40 Luxurious
43 A long way to go?
46 "Give __ break!"
49 Manual offerings
50 Hurler Hershiser
51 Clemson athlete
53 Indian whose tribe's name means "lovers of sexual pleasure"
54 Fastening device
56 Thoughtful sort
58 Slammer
59 First word in Massachusetts' motto
60 Utopias
61 ". . . __ saw Elba"
62 Gulf capital
63 Back to zero, perhaps
64 Reddish-brown gem
65 Whipping site at sea

DOWN
1 Luce and others
2 Truncate
3 Impotent
4 Anthony Quinn title role
5 Semitic lang.
6 Magnetite, e.g.
7 Fruity liqueur
8 Like an old pay telephone call
9 Stat for which Cecil Fielder once led the A.L.
10 West end?
11 Summer game
12 Church recitation
13 Start of TV Guide listings
21 Bug-eyed monsters
22 Stag party staple
26 In every respect
29 Couples grp.
30 A.C. measure
33 Account, in a way
34 Disposition
35 They may be cross
36 Angers
37 Demolitionist's supply
38 Its symbol is an omega
40 Expresses
41 Pseudo fat
42 Less clear, as river water
44 Milit. rank
45 Milit. school
46 Where Kampala is
47 Physiological pentad
48 Eager
52 Skyscraper construction unit
54 Start for while
55 Crocus or freesia, e.g.
57 Wind dir.

ACROSS

1 Make silly
6 Undergoes
9 Out of cards in a suit
13 Peter __ Tchaikovsky
14 Common-sense
15 River through Aragón
16 Ballgoer
17 Puling
19 Happy spymaster?
21 Heartfelt
22 Record-owning
25 Poolroom aid
26 "And thereby hangs __"
28 A party to
29 Kind of beer
30 Interpretation
31 Summoned
32 Happy Wagner hero?
35 Trekkie idol
38 Province
39 Subject of academic study
42 Viking deity
43 Hodgepodge
45 __ spumante
46 Certain riding horses
48 Like many gardens
50 Happy ex-Mayor of New York?
52 Play backup for
54 Make fit
56 "Damn Yankees" vamp
57 Plunked items
58 Eugene who wrote "Wynken, Blynken and Nod"
59 58-Across, e.g.

60 Minster seat
61 Business concern

DOWN

1 Dribble guard
2 Like a Thomas Gray work
3 Schoolmaster's order
4 Word of the hour?
5 Yonder
6 Doubter's outbursts
7 Member of a very old kingdom
8 Dotty, perhaps
9 Antonio or Bassanio, e.g.

10 Complaint
11 Investigator's employer: Abbr.
12 Hairstyles
14 Hon
18 Inadequately
20 Boardroom easel display
21 __ Lanka
23 Miney follower
24 Omega
27 Year's record
30 Modern ink source
31 Singer Zadora
32 Item aboard a merchant ship
33 Awards for Sheryl Crow

34 Overhaul a soundtrack
35 Jean, for one
36 Witness's reply
37 Wonderwork
39 Pequod hand
40 Bell site
41 Prefix with life or wife
43 Grab
44 Tremulous
45 Park in Maine
47 Issue matériel
49 Toronto Maple __
51 Resurgently
52 Swiss eminence
53 Pigeon sound
55 Kingdome scores, for short

41 AMHERST OBSERVATION by Richard Hughes

ACROSS
1 Tries to take (out)
5 Mischievous
10 Novelist Mario Vargas Llosa's home
14 Carnival tune
15 Actor Greene
16 40's foe
17 Think of it!
18 Swiftly
19 Nicaragua's second-largest city
20 Start of a quote from Emily Dickinson
23 Direction in music
24 Picks up readings on
25 Poet's preposition
27 Indoor-outdoor rooms
31 Common street name
34 Part 2 of the quote
39 Feeding time sound
41 Set of beliefs
42 Initial offering?
43 Part 3 of the quote
46 John __ Passos
47 Time for a coffee break, maybe
48 Lunch on
50 Rags
55 Esteem
59 End of the quote
62 Tel __
63 Run with one's mouth open?
64 Arab chieftain
65 Strike out
66 Not wait one's turn
67 Communion, e.g.

68 It's unique
69 Transport
70 Opposite of 65-Across

DOWN
1 You may assume it
2 Move somewhat furtively
3 Certain movie light: Var.
4 Michelangelo's "Pietà," e.g.
5 Overseas carrier
6 Runs
7 Formulate
8 Like some ancient ruins
9 Exigencies
10 Athletic training site, in Greek antiquity
11 Divorcées
12 Portuguese rivers
13 American mil. wing
21 Actress Garr
22 Certain tide
26 Postal letters?
28 Peel
29 Division word
30 Seeming eternity
31 Spew
32 __-majesté
33 Cut
35 Italian number
36 Stag goers

37 Old Tokyo
38 A little
40 "Anything you say"
44 Eclipse, maybe
45 Overhang
49 Selfish ones
51 "Is that __?!"
52 Frère's sister
53 Verdi aria
54 Zeno follower
56 Restrict
57 Join
58 Plume's source
59 Flat
60 Revolting
61 "Baywatch" type
62 Foofaraw

ACROSS
1 African scourge
7 Stepping
15 Ultimatum word
16 Orderly place
17 Takes in, for example
18 Trenchant
19 Light on the set: Var.
20 "It's no __!"
21 Volcanic elements
22 These might cover fires
25 Amigos
26 Verdi masterpiece, with "La"
29 Concert prop
31 "__ Said" (Neil Diamond hit)
32 Agcy. issuance
33 October handout
36 Quick hands artist
40 "Have __ day"
41 __-Magnon
42 Tooth part
43 Integration symbol
44 Lower jaw
46 Black shade
49 1951 Giant hero
51 "__ moi . . ."
53 Some clock-radios, or their settings
54 Quick
58 Food poisoning
60 You can count on it
61 Jerry Seinfeld contemporary
62 Stomach corrosion
63 Least sufficient
64 Sofa type

DOWN
1 Shipbuilding wood
2 Shades' stopping point
3 Suffix with disk
4 H.G. Wells's mad scientist
5 Composer Rachmaninoff
6 Hesitant sounds
7 Favorite 60's song of 36-Across?
8 Actress Blakley
9 Computer key: Abbr.
10 Make __ of oneself
11 Favorite feat of 4-Down?
12 "__ far, far better thing . . ."
13 This may be contemplated
14 Daly's TV co-star
20 You, in the Yucatán
23 Most cautious
24 Olympic roster
26 Longtime Capitol Hill nickname
27 __ avis
28 Revival word
30 "D.C. Cab" actor
34 From __ (opening bit)
35 Drive (along)
37 Fort Worth sch.
38 Lab units
39 Homophone of 42-Across: Abbr.
45 Within reach
46 Melville's Vere and others: Abbr.
47 Instrument's lens
48 Bakery attraction
50 Big name in briefs
52 1972 agreement, for short
55 "Rhyme Pays" rapper
56 Bait, sometimes
57 Actual being
59 View on the Seine
60 Out of: Ger.

43 ADHERENCE by Susan Smith

ACROSS

1 Convince with smooth talk
5 Wallop but good
9 Like some pans
13 __ lot (few)
14 Architect Saarinen
15 Is beholden to
16 Show authority, in a saying
19 Native of Novi Sad
20 Classic party activity
21 Rumpus
23 Sacred image: Var.
24 Fare-well link
25 Stay for a while
28 Reflects
32 Six-time U.S. Open tennis champ
33 Bistro
34 Divinity school subj.
35 Unaccounted-for combatants: Abbr.
36 Main impact of an attack
38 The Destroyer, in Hinduism
39 Danube city
40 Tom-tom
41 Traffic jam
42 Word with fruit or play
44 Famous park name, once
46 Baby sounds
47 Salve ingredient
48 Charm
51 Caverns
55 1948 film "The Fallen __"
56 Be substantial, as a meal
58 Combustible heap
59 Two-dimensional extent
60 "The wolf __ the door"
61 Slave to detail
62 Where oysters hang out
63 Parker and Waterman

DOWN

1 60's civil rights grp.
2 Beery of 20's-40's films
3 __ vez (again): Sp.
4 Soldiers
5 Precise
6 Fix, as a paper clip
7 "Trinity" novelist
8 Slough
9 More intrusive
10 John Irving's "A Prayer for __ Meany"
11 Square, updated
12 Is loyal to
17 People of eastern Siberia
18 It's not automatic
22 "Present"
24 Govt. agent
25 Heist words
26 St. Teresa of __
27 Paper measures
29 Bay window
30 Variety show
31 Comedy type
33 Diploma word
36 Halloween transport
37 Box score column
38 Itinerary diversion
40 New Look designer
41 Certain investment, for short
43 Fishmonger's tool
44 Hauled
45 Island greetings
48 Crankcase item
49 Romantic interlude
50 Hurting
51 Skirt panel
52 French river
53 Israeli diplomat
54 Atl. speedsters
57 Check

44 HIT THE SPA by David J. Kahn

ACROSS

1 Not occurring naturally
7 Beach resort near San Diego
13 Unfortunate landing spot for a parachutist
15 Fabric border
16 Workout expert
18 Bon __
19 Not exactly PG-rated
20 Dos halved
21 Court wear
23 Incite
24 There was much of this in Shakespeare
25 Lilly of Lilly Pharmaceutical
26 Former N.B.A. venue, with "the"
28 Acclaim
30 H.M.O. employee
31 "Midnight Cowboy" role
33 "A bird," "a plane" or "Superman" preceder
34 Decorator, e.g.
38 Tic-tac-toe failure
39 Where the United Nations' setup was discussed
40 Pilot's announcement, for short
43 Insolent look
45 Bygone leader
46 Mo. to celebrate National Clown Week
47 Blacken
48 Actress MacDowell
51 Man with a mission
53 Abbr. after a comma
54 More urbane
56 "Tasty!"
57 Workout incentive
61 Most lenient
62 Rat
63 Ornate
64 It had many missions

DOWN

1 "The Racer's Edge"
2 Diva's device
3 Workout activity
4 "Beau __"
5 W.W. II command
6 Family figures?
7 Skin: Prefix
8 Comedienne Boosler
9 Year in Nero's reign
10 Workout machine
11 Hidden items, sometimes
12 Transplant
14 How obvious? Very much so!
15 Solo, in a way
17 Kind of aide
21 Flushed
22 Gather on a surface, chemically
27 Fannie or Ginnie follower
29 Cannes co.
32 Sesames
35 Howard of comedy
36 D.C.'s Union __
37 Irish national symbol
38 Rampaging
41 Hurly-burly
42 Sit in the cellar
43 Liquored up
44 Nonvolcanic eruptions
49 Cuckoo
50 Old Dodge model
52 Reply in a children's argument
55 Actress Lee of TV and film
58 Grunts, so to speak
59 "Bear"
60 Modernist, for short

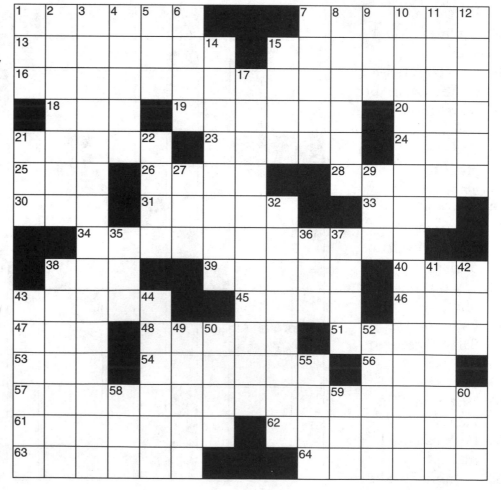

ACROSS

1 *"Toil and trouble" preceder*
7 *Normal, in a way*
13 The N. Platte, e.g.
15 Less sound
16 Increaser of one's growth potential?
17 Gifts
18 Pub supply
19 Garments for granny
21 Nintendo's Super __
22 Tito's homeland
24 Slalom segment
27 Like some arches
28 Car part
29 Taxonomic div.
32 Willingly
33 Composer Mahler
35 "__ Male War Bride" (1949 movie)
37 Sound units: Abbr.
39 Fin de __ (remainder): Fr.
40 Marinated beef strip
42 Official records
44 Cape __
45 Some boxing wins
46 "The Thrill Is Gone" singer
48 "__ out!"
49 Adriatic port
50 Typewriter key
53 Pieces
54 "Qué __ es?" (Spanish 101 question)
55 Sneakers brand
58 Made of certain twigs
61 Many a Miamian
62 Corporate routine
63 *1990's sitcom*
64 *Name in the news, 6/5/68*

DOWN

1 *English pop group*
2 *"__ Mio"*
3 Spurs
4 *It's unfair*
5 Year in Nero's reign
6 Poetic contraction
7 Out of the freezer
8 *Home of Whitman College*
9 Squeezes (out)
10 Writer Anaïs
11 Hanoi festival
12 Age: Abbr.
14 Cobbled
15 *What each star represents*
20 Like the answers to this puzzle's 12 italicized clues?
22 B
23 BBC's Italian counterpart
24 *Newsboy's cry*
25 Assassinated
26 *Height of the N.B.A.'s Gheorghe Muresan*
28 Peer Gynt's mother
29 *Evenly split*
30 Open-eyed
31 *"Catch-22" character*
34 Strunk & White subject
36 Family member
38 Clip
41 Rubber
43 Cable choice
47 Short hair, to Burns
49 *"It'll be O.K."*
50 The Bible before Joshua
51 Asian palm
52 *European resort*
53 Burlesque bit
54 Münster Mister
55 Duos: Abbr.
56 Defendants at law
57 Nail-biters: Abbr.
59 Eur. carrier
60 "Lord, is __?"

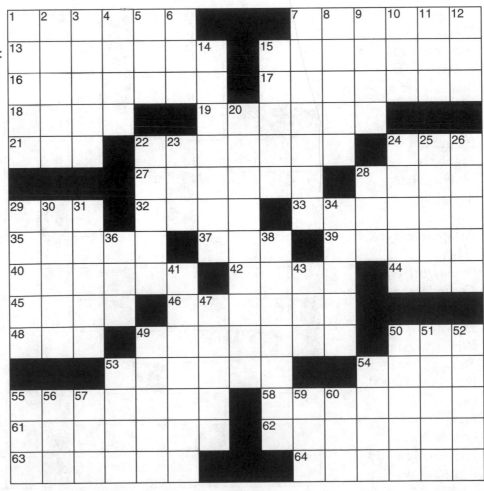

46 TEAMMATES by David J. Kahn

ACROSS

1. Construction lifts
7. "If __ a nickel . . ."
11. Pointed criticism
14. You can say that again!
15. Section flanked by aisles
16. Hubbub
17. Appoint
18. Spring zoo attraction
20. Tick off
21. Dearie
22. Ambles (along)
23. Magellan, e.g.
27. Crescent-shaped figure
28. Olive __
29. Beach time in Buenos Aires
32. Retired
33. Struggle
34. O'Brien of "The Barefoot Contessa"
36. TV news time
37. Namesakes of a literary fox
39. Suffix with saw
40. Plain homes
42. Eight pts.
43. Not occurring naturally
44. __ voce
45. Adaptable truck, for short
46. Stonewort, e.g.
47. Confederate soldier, at times?
50. Pundit
53. Where to hear "All Things Considered"
54. Number of articles in the Constitution
55. New York City opera benefactor?
57. Melon originally from Turkey
60. Tide rival
61. Noted first name in jazz
62. Like Alban Berg's music
63. Get spliced
64. __-poly
65. Metric units

DOWN

1. Med. care provider
2. Sweep
3. World's fair pavilion
4. Famished
5. Tot's transport
6. Start of many Western place names
7. Theme of this puzzle
8. 1492 Columbus discovery
9. Dow Jones fig.
10. Pool areas
11. Item in a trunk
12. Together, musically
13. Feints in boxing
19. "Air Music" composer
21. Contribute, as to an account
23. Criticize in no uncertain terms
24. Red corundums
25. Continues
26. Razzed
30. Louis XIV, to himself?
31. Wound up
35. Cheerless
37. Attorney's request
38. Critic
41. Old words from which modern words are derived
43. Half of the Odd Couple
48. Sound of passage
49. Not perfectly round
50. Fish-eating duck
51. Ginger Rogers tune "__ in the Money"
52. Not much
56. Day-__
57. Be-bopper
58. "Phooey!"
59. Capp and Capone

ACROSS

1 Delete, in a way
4 Low blow?
8 Glacial ridge
13 Run of the ranch?
14 Riyadh resident
15 "__ crying over spilt milk"
16 Alpine aster
18 Pound
19 Kind of show
20 Radical
21 Fluid container
22 Baryshnikov's former co.
25 __-Magnon
26 Attach, as a patch
28 Antwerp artisan
30 Saw in the direction of the grain
31 Jackie's second
32 Game plan
34 Pitching credit
35 Saki story
38 __ Thai (official name of Thailand)
39 Unskilled writer
40 67-Across employee
41 Stupidity
43 Went underground
44 Rhoda's mom
45 Eskimo's environs
49 Corrida cheer
50 __ deferens
51 Pilot's heading
52 God whose symbol was two horses' heads
53 Three on a match?
55 Model Campbell
57 Rod with a racquet
58 Distinguished politicians
62 Concerning
63 A head of Time
64 A head of France
65 They make a mint
66 Epitome of 41-Across
67 Tax agcy.

DOWN

1 Group of signs
2 Instant impression
3 Former Rhode Island Senator
4 __ kwon do
5 One of the Four Forest Cantons
6 __-relief
7 Bodybuilder's pride
8 Degree of randomness, in science
9 It's near Piccadilly
10 "Seven Samurai" director
11 Arcane
12 Yankee's foe
13 1988 Peter Allen musical
17 Doc's best friend
20 Brigs, e.g.
23 Where the U.S.S. Cyclops disappeared
24 Shocks
25 "Rambo" actor Richard and kin
27 Flirtatious signal
29 Prufrock creator's initials
33 Bill
35 Canyon feature
36 Mike Hammer's creator
37 Restyled
39 33d Pres.
41 Distracts
42 Public to-do
46 Fraternal twin, in chemistry
47 Bill Haley's backup
48 Round-Manhattan cruise company
54 Outlet
56 Wine region
57 Varnish ingredient
58 __-pitch softball
59 Formal wear, informally
60 Crackerjack
61 Part of a royal flush

48 LEAKY TIRE by Rose White

ACROSS

1 Unposed photo
7 Streisand, in fanzines
11 Cpl.'s superior
14 Tom, Dick or Harry
15 Year in Henry I's reign
16 Court
17 Military meal manager
19 Set off
20 Used a sauna
21 What "bathy-" means
23 Homeboys' "fraternity"
24 Consulate's kin
25 Somewhat firm
28 Track tournaments
29 Woolen cloth
30 Homes of the rich and famous
33 Beauty preceder?
34 Epoch
35 Hieroglyphic stone locale
40 Musical counterpoint
44 Prison guard, in slang
45 Air shafts for mines
46 Lewd
48 Sweep with binoculars
49 Decapitates
50 Hearty?
54 Clockmaker Terry
55 Embroidery style
57 Kind of camera: Abbr.
58 Margarita garnish
59 Author Welty
60 Grab a bite
61 "Waiting for the Robert __"
62 Let live

DOWN

1 Rotating engine parts
2 Over
3 Amex alternative
4 Pharmacist's concerns
5 Coffee choice
6 Diplomat's quest
7 Mercedes competitor
8 University environment
9 Ancient galleys
10 Auxiliary wager
11 Diner entrée
12 Al et al.
13 Hungarian wine
18 Nosed (out)
22 __-cake (baby's game)
25 "Suppose they gave __ ..."
26 Sign of the Times?
27 Tuxedo accompaniment
31 River to Donegal Bay
32 Hurdles for srs.
36 Behold, to Pilate
37 Something cloying
38 Plant runner
39 Absolutely fabulous
40 Platters
41 Covers completely
42 Nascent company
43 Shaw play
46 Corpulent
47 Italian's word of approval
51 "Ripley's Believe __ Not!"
52 4,047 square meters
53 Neighbor of Nigeria
56 Bishop's jurisdiction

ACROSS

1 Site of this puzzle's thematic features
5 Nixon's running mate in 1960
10 Nibble
14 Crowning
15 Bee-fitting description?
16 Bone: Prefix
17 Red Skelton persona
18 Stood for
19 Épouse's mate
20 Perform, as one's duties
22 Colorado, e.g.
23 Is rather like Rather
25 Shaking
28 U.S.D.A. power agcy.
29 Pizarro's prize
30 Juicy fruit
37 Pig's place
39 Els with tees
40 Yeats's land
41 Courtroom figures
43 "Hurrah!"
44 Comics word spelled between asterisks
45 Lucifer and Pansy's boy
47 Noted band conductor
54 "Henry & June" character
55 They give a ship increased speed
59 Orch. section
60 Cat's eyes, at times
61 Torment
62 Rectangular pier
63 "Le __ du printemps"
64 Arthur of "Hoop Dreams"
65 Present time
66 Glacial formation
67 When the French go en vacances

DOWN

1 King of Saudi Arabia
2 Yours, in Tours
3 Pens' mates
4 Long stretches
5 Prayer wheel users
6 Beethoven wrote just one
7 Identify
8 Thief, in Yiddish
9 Fangorn Forest dweller
10 Put forward
11 River to the Missouri
12 Float accessory
13 They get what's coming to them
21 It's pitched on a field
22 Old buffalo hunter
24 Heraldic bands
25 Thimble Theater star
26 Queued up
27 Hel raiser?
30 Tree with triangular nuts
31 __ artium (logic): Lat.
32 Clinic workers, for short
33 Kind of dye
34 1982 Boxleitner film
35 Nap
36 Breadwinner
38 Peculiar to a population
42 Lifts
45 Fathead
46 Sheepish reply?
47 Black lacquer
48 Bridge bid, informally
49 Creator of Truthful James
50 Mallorca y Menorca
51 Purse item
52 Eccentric
53 Andretti adversary
56 Cassio's rival
57 Place
58 "Don't delete this"
60 Compass point

ACROSS

1 Start to form, as a storm
5 "__-Dick"
9 Christie's Miss Marple
13 Exude
14 Village Voice award
15 Miser Marner
17 Where this answer goes
19 Singing syllable
20 Mysterious loch
21 Utah mountains
22 Villa d'__
23 Up to the task
24 Goodyear fleet
27 Train storage area
31 W.W. II hero Murphy
32 Seas, to Cousteau
33 Go a-courtin'
35 What this answer does
38 Suffix with ranch
39 " . . . unto us __ is given"
40 Contemptible one
41 Narrow-necked bottle
44 Cried like a baby
45 Word with slicker or hall
46 Guns, as an engine
47 "Lucky" dice rolls
50 __ over (carry through)
51 Point of decline
55 What this answer seems to have
57 Book with legends
58 The triple in a triple play
59 Author Bagnold
60 Exude
61 Phoenix neighbor
62 Thanksgiving dishes

DOWN

1 Ring engagement
2 First sound in an M-G-M film
3 Poet Pound
4 Little piggy's cry
5 Some MOMA paintings
6 More than plump
7 Strained pea catchers
8 Biblical affirmative
9 Small bus
10 Heaps
11 Cape Canaveral org.
12 Gentlemen: Abbr.
15 Expertise
16 Without obligation
18 Picasso-Braque movement
22 Bahrain bigwig
23 Hammerin' Hank
24 Bundled, as straw
25 Riches
26 Manner of speaking
27 Scouting mission
28 Horrendous
29 Stir from slumber
30 Parceled (out)
32 Like fine netting
34 Chinese philosopher
36 Football team quorum
37 Starts a crop
42 Polar feature
43 Mr. __ (Pixie and Dixie's nemesis)
44 Mythological woman with unruly hair
46 Laughfests
47 Mineral springs
48 Suffix with cigar
49 Reprehensible
50 Veracious
51 Sicilian peak
52 Cup lip
53 Political campaigns
54 Mr. Turkey
56 Susan of "Looker"

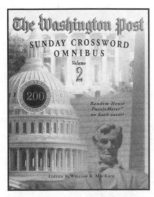

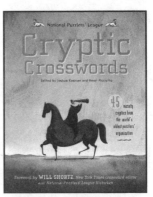

ANSWERS

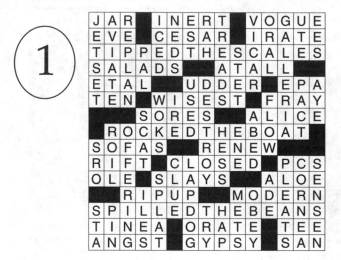

1

```
J A R   I N E R T   V O G U E
E V E   C E S A R   I R A T E
T I P P E D T H E S C A L E S
S A L A D S   A T A L L
E T A L   U D D E R   E P A
T E N   W I S E S T   F R A Y
      S O R E S   A L I C E
  R O C K E D T H E B O A T
S O F A S   R E N E W
R I F T   C L O S E D   P C S
O L E   S L A Y S   A L O E
    R I P U P   M O D E R N
S P I L L E D T H E B E A N S
T I N E A   O R A T E   T E E
A N G S T   G Y P S Y   S A N
```

2

```
J A G S   B A S I S   C E D E
O G R E   E R I C A   A X E L
I R O N M A I D E N   S P A M
S E P T E T   E D I T I O N S
T E E   N I A   T A N S
      P U T T E R A R O U N D
A D D I S   T R U R O   R O Y
L I O N   D E R B Y   F E T E
P E W   M A N O R   R O S E S
S U N D A Y D R I V E R
    G O L D   C I A   E S C
S O R C E R E R   S C A M P I
T H A T   E L I J A H W O O D
U N D O   A L O N G   E T R E
B O E R   M E T R E   S E E R
```

3

```
G O A L S ■ B A E R ■ T H U S
R I V E T ■ O U S E ■ W A N E
A L O N E ■ C L A D ■ I B I D
D Y N A M I C D U O ■ N I T E
■ ■ M R E ■ L I T T E R ■ ■
■ A N D E S ■ A C E T O ■ ■
C R E E D ■ S L A N T W I S E
O A H U ■ G R I S T ■ E N T O
S P I C E R A C K ■ U R G E S
■ ■ E R A S E ■ I N S E T ■
L A R S E N ■ U L M ■ ■ ■
A V O W ■ D O U B L E P L A Y
K I W I ■ A R N O ■ A L E V E
E L A L ■ M A T A ■ N O V E L
S A N D ■ S L O T ■ T W I R L
```

4

```
P I E S ■ T E M P E ■ C H E R
A N A T ■ E V E R Y ■ R A T E
S P R Y ■ R E N E E ■ I R A N
T U T ■ V E N U S D E M I L O
A T H E I S T ■ R A E ■ ■
■ A N N A ■ C R O S S S E A
M O N D E ■ E R U P T ■ A R C
E G G S ■ A R I E S ■ S T A R
A G E ■ A B I E S ■ M O U S E
L I L A B N E R ■ C A R R ■
■ C O O ■ B A N A N A S
M E R C U R Y L Y N X ■ N R A
O L E O ■ M A I N E ■ D I E T
O M A R ■ A L T E R ■ A N N O
G O L D ■ L E E R S ■ D E A N
```

5

```
C M O N ■ E L L A ■ S A C R E
R O P E ■ D U E T ■ A C R E S
A N E W ■ M A S T ■ M E A N T
M A D A B O U T Y O U ■ C E E
■ ■ R O N ■ S T R I K E S
B A C K S T O P ■ C A N E ■
O U R ■ C O M A S ■ I N D I A
A R A B ■ N I N E S ■ S I B S
R A Z E S ■ T E P E E ■ C A P
■ Y A N G ■ S T A R T E R S
S E Q U I N S ■ C I O ■
A S U ■ C U C K O O C L O C K
S T I C K ■ A L K A ■ E L L E
H A L L E ■ M E L S ■ D E A N
A S T I R ■ P E A T ■ O O P S
```

6

```
S W A G S ■ S C U P ■ C R O C
A P L E A ■ E R N E ■ H E R O
M A L T L I Q U O R ■ I T E M
■ U N T R U E ■ M E N A G E
D E V O ■ M E L T I N G P O T
A R I ■ B A L ■ O T T ■ E N O
G A U Z E ■ E M M E T ■ ■
■ M I L T O N B E R L E ■
■ P A R E D ■ E C L A T
I R E ■ T A I ■ A D D ■ O L E
M O L T E N L A V A ■ U N I T
B O U N D S ■ B A L I N G ■
I N D O ■ M U L T I G R A I N
B E E T ■ I D E A ■ O U T R E
E Y R E ■ T E R R ■ R H E T T
```

7

```
C H I C ■ M I N U S ■ D O T
H A L O ■ A T O N E S ■ E V E
E L K S ■ N E T H E R ■ T A X
F E A S T O R F A M I N E ■
■ E A R ■ A M S ■ O R A L
G E S T E ■ S I P ■ T E R R A
R A H S ■ M O R E O R L E S S
I T O ■ M O M ■ R A Y ■ N O S
N O W O R N E V E R ■ A C N E
D U C T S ■ W E D ■ P R E S S
S T A T ■ S H E ■ U A R ■
■ S O O N E R O R L A T E R
L E I ■ R A R I N G ■ Y A L E
O W N ■ G R E E C E ■ E C O N
B E G ■ E S S E S ■ D O N T
```

8

```
T A X I ■ S P A C E ■ H U M E
O X E N ■ O R S O N ■ A Z O V
N E R D ■ L A I R D ■ Y I P E
G L O O M A N D D O O M ■ ■
■ L O C K E ■ A O R T A
S T P E T E ■ A W K W A R D
P A I N E ■ M A N E ■ T A D
H U S T L E A N D B U S T L E
E R A ■ X R A Y ■ P A L E R
R U N B A C K ■ R E N E E S
E S S E S ■ B L I N D ■
■ S H A K E A N D B A K E
C H A T ■ B E L T S ■ A V I D
A U T O ■ C N O T E ■ N O T I
P H E W ■ S O W E D ■ K N E E
```

9

```
A B B E . C A R A . M I L L E
W E A K . U P O N . A D A I R
A L B E R T S O N . N E W E R
R O B . H I E D . D E A R .
D I L L I E S . S E S T E T S
S T E I N . C H I . E N I D
. K E R O U A C . C P A
B A N E . A D O R E . D E S K
E L I . D E M P S E Y .
T A C T . I T O . R A M B O
E S K I M O S . T O A D I E D
. L E A S . F A S T . A T E
E M A I L . N I C H O L S O N
G A U N T . O D I E . A M O S
G A S S Y . B E T A . B A K E
```

10

```
F R I J O L E S . D A R T E R
E N S E N A D A . E N R O L L
M A R A T H O N . E D S E L S
. N O R M A N D Y .
S C R I P . B E S T B O Y
T H E E . O U N C E . O A K S
L A B . S I T U . A P R I L
. L I T T L E B I G H O R N .
B O R E D . I R A S . I A M
A N T S . T S A R S . P E W S
A S H T R A Y . S A R A S
. Y O R K T O W N .
Y E H U D I . A N T I E T A M
E R A S E S . N U R S L I N G
R E W A R M . S T A S S E N S
```

11

```
A T O M . F O R M S . N A S A
D I V E . E L I S E . I N O N
D R A W B R I D G E A H E A D
S O L . L A V E . D M I T R I
. C O L E . U T I L .
A P A R T . S A T I N . G O B
S E T A T . S A M . I R A E
K E E P O F F T H E G R A S S
E L I S . I L E . R A D I O
D E N . E V E R S . A T E S T
. S T E W . H O T E .
S E D A N S . B I T E . G A L
P R I V A T E E N T R A N C E
E I N E . A G A T E . M A M A
D E A R . R O T O R . S T E P
```

12

```
R B I S . C O L O N . R O M A
A L O E . O R A T E . U K E S
P U N C T U A T I O N M A R K
. E S T O P . S N A P P L E
. M E T S . S L I E R
L I C I T . I N V I T E .
O R O N O . N E E R . P I P
P A N A M A C A N A L C I T Y
E N E . S A K I . E A S E L
. I R E N I C . A W A R E
A E T N A . N E I N .
T R O T T E D . S T E A K
I N T E S T I N A L O R G A N
L I E N . A N O D E . G O R E
T E S T . L O R D S . O G L E
```

13

```
C A M A Y . A L E U T . M A R
O H A R E . B I L K O . I C E
P A N T S P O C K E T . S H A
. D A R K . E N S O R
D I L B E R T . J I B B O O M
U V U L A S . B A T A A N
P A C E R . S O B I G . E F T
E N I D . G L O B S . T S A R
S A L . L L A M A . T A C K Y
. L A Y U P S . V E N U E S
P R E L I M S . D E S S E R T
R A B I N . A I N T .
O V A . G I M M E A B R E A K
B E L . T R A I T . A D D L E
E L L . O K I E S . N A T T Y
```

14

```
S I L O . B A L S A . S H O P
O R A L . A S I A N . P A N E
H A N D I N H A N D . O R C A
O N E . S T E M . E M O T E R
. A L E S . C R A F T .
A M B L E R . L O S T S O U L
D E L I S . C A N O E . H B O
A L O T . R O U E N . G A O L
M E W . B E R R Y . C O R A L
N E B R A S K A . C H A T T Y
. Y O K E S . F O A L
E M B L E M . A L L I . S O B
V I L A . B L U E O N B L U E
I R O N . L A D E N . I O T A
L E W D . E D I T S . T E S T
```

15

```
SAYS ■ AWACS ■ ARID
UTAH ■ ZEBRA ■ SORE
EASYSTREET ■ SCAN
TRINI ■ ETTA ■ UKES
■ IRENE ■ SENTRY ■
■ SEAM ■ HERBS
RAHS ■ GARAGE ■ OAK
USA ■ MAHATMA ■ ALI
MIR ■ ENIGMA ■ ODDS
SADAT ■ STIR ■
■ DRAMAS ■ SMASH
HARI ■ ALAW ■ OCCUR
ASIS ■ NATHANLANE
HAVE ■ INEED ■ ELAN
APES ■ CASTS ■ SEND
```

16

```
CUBE ■ SLASH ■ PIPE
APEX ■ MAINE ■ OVID
PORTLANDOR ■ CANI
ENG ■ URGE ■ ORANGE
■ ARTE ■ ICET ■
SMILEY ■ PROCESS
WILLS ■ GOOP ■ LEMA
ALOE ■ NOONS ■ LOAN
TENN ■ ONLY ■ COULD
■ RATINGS ■ REILLY
■ ONUS ■ WARD ■
AVOWER ■ AARE ■ WOE
NEON ■ BETHESDAMD
CAPP ■ ALTOS ■ ORIG
ELSA ■ NONOT ■ ANTE
```

17

```
SLAP ■ ANJOU ■ CHAW
PANE ■ LEARN ■ RARA
ASTI ■ BANFF ■ EVEN
THEGRATEFULDEAD
■ NANO ■ REO ■
RATON ■ MERE ■ FOB
APHID ■ ZERO ■ ROUE
MERRYWIDOWWALTZ
PROS ■ AGES ■ ASIDE
SSW ■ URSA ■ STOOL
■ SRI ■ HAHA ■
KILLINGMESOFTLY
ERIE ■ ENERO ■ ASIA
MARE ■ SATON ■ RANK
PSAT ■ STANG ■ IRKS
```

18

```
BASH ■ PLEB ■ LAPIN
UPTO ■ LAIR ■ ALONE
BRER ■ ATNO ■ RILKE
BORNINKENTUCKY
ANN ■ NNE ■ CREE ■
■ ITE ■ OHO ■ DAM
RAISEDININDIANA
OGDEN ■ NEA ■ RODDY
LIVEDINILLINOIS
ONE ■ TOL ■ OVA ■
■ DCCV ■ LGE ■ PEA
■ ABRAHAMLINCOLN
SHOOT ■ TEAC ■ ANEW
SONIC ■ ERMA ■ ETNA
WYETH ■ SEAL ■ NEAR
```

19

```
WORD ■ DIMS ■ SHEBA
IDIO ■ EPEE ■ PINED
SANG ■ AHME ■ EPODE
PYGMALION ■ APSES
■ ALEG ■ AFRO ■
RES ■ DRED ■ ASLANT
ARENA ■ NEED ■ YEAR
ZOLA ■ SINUS ■ TRIO
ODER ■ MAIM ■ GAILY
RESCUE ■ MESO ■ ESS
■ ITES ■ NAGS ■
WORST ■ PHILOMELA
ANISE ■ LEDA ■ OMAR
LEMUR ■ IRED ■ TINE
TRESS ■ TOSS ■ ERAS
```

20

```
BOTH ■ JIHAD ■ SKIM
AURA ■ ADELA ■ ANNO
BRINGMEAUNICORN
ASONE ■ ALMAS ■ CEO
■ ANT ■ SNEAK ■
HIGHERUP ■ GERARD
ISR ■ VISOR ■ OBOE
TEENAGEWEREWOLF
IRAE ■ SENOR ■ UFO
TETHER ■ REPARTEE
■ FIXES ■ ESE ■
UMA ■ ENLAI ■ ELATE
RELUCTANTDRAGON
GALS ■ AVOIR ■ CORD
ELSA ■ LENNY ■ EGOS
```

21

```
A S A P   F A D E   A N D G O
D A V E   I L E X   S I R E D
S C A R   L O B E   S T Y N E
      J A M E S S T E W A R T
A B D U L       I R I S E S
G E O R G E C S C O T T
A R T Y   S H E A   S A M S
I L E   S I N C E   H A P
N E R O   L O T S   L A R A
    F R E D R I C M A R C H
E S S A I S     A D D O N
S P E N C E R T R A C Y
T O R A H   A E O N   B A T S
O S A G E   C A S T   U H O H
P A L E R   K L E E   G A M Y
```

22

```
A L A   S P A S M   F A S T
V I N   T E S L A   A T E A M
E T A   O R I O N   Z O R R O
R E L I V I N G T H E P A S T
  R Y N E       R O D   P U T
M A Z E   U N M A N   A H S O
A T E   O N E A   O H M
B I R T H D A Y P R E S E N T
    H O E   A K E Y   P A R
M A R X   R A N G E   S I Z E
O R A   S G T   P I C A
B A C K T O T H E F U T U R E
I R E N E   A A R O N   R E A
L A M E R   C L I N K   E T S
  T E E N   K E N T S   S H Y
```

23

```
R E C   S H A W L   A C E R B
E A R   T A L I A   L A T E X
P R E S I D E N T O F I R A Q
O T T E R     K E A N U
S H A Q   S K I E R S   S O O
T A N   B A R Q S   S C A M
    A U D I T   T A T A R S
  Q A N D A S E S S I O N S
A T R E S T   S C A L P
R I O T   S T A R S   P C T
C P U   A T E S T S   A E R O
  S E N O R   Q A T A R
Q W E R T Y K E Y B O A R D S
E E R I E   I C E U P   E L O
D E S K S   N O T C H   L E S
```

24

```
S A L A D   C O L E   P A P
I R A N I   O R E L   H U R L
P A S T A   N A G S   I N C A
    I N A C L A I R E D A Y
C B S   E V E   T E E   I N E
O R E O   A R G O   O A T E R
C A M P S I T E   T P K
A N I T A L O O S W E I G H T
    I V S   D A I N T I E R
B O C C I   F E R N   A S I A
R I O   O S U   A G E   T R Y
A L H I R T M Y S E L F
K E E N   A B O O   F A Z E D
E R R S   G L U T   I R A T E
S S E   S E R A   N E P A L
```

25

```
C Y S T   O Z A W A   N A R C
R A T E   M A R I N   I N K Y
A L I A   A S I D E   G O O D
W I L M A R U D O L P H
L E T U S     W E A T H E R
    P O P P A   S C A R E
L A P   F R E D A S T A I R E
O D E A   E L O P E   P R O D
B A R N E Y F R A N K   Y R S
E M P T Y   E R T E S
D E S I R E S   M O U N T
    B E T T Y C R O C K E R
J O J O   H O O E Y   C A S E
O V I D   A N G L E   E S T A
B A B Y   N E A L S   R E S T
```

26

```
S A S S   I D L E S   P L A Y
A R L O   B O I S E   R E N E
H E A D S E T T E R   O C T A
L A P   C R E E   E S T H E R
    W E I R   I N T O
F A R I N A     C R E S C E N T
O P I N E   G A O L   O L I O
R A N G   R U N N Y   L U N A
E R G S   E Y E S   O L D A S
S T O P O V E R   D R I E S T
    A P E D   H A T E
P L A N A R   S O P H   S E N
R A N I   S H A M P O O D L E
O K I E   E A S E L   T A M S
D E L L   S T E R E   T K O S
```

27

```
LUNGS ■ PAW ■ IBSEN
OPERA ■ ALA ■ NITRO
CREAK ■ NOV ■ CLING
KIDSINTHEHALL ■ ■
USES ■ OHARAS ■ EBB
PED ■ POE ■ SWELTER
■ ■ HANOI ■ ■ ATTA
INNOCENTSABROAD
NOEL ■ ■ SKULK ■
DOWERED ■ EDT ■ QTS
OKS ■ USABLE ■ PURE
■ CHILDRENSHOUR
BRAIN ■ GAT ■ TOTEM
AISLE ■ UVA ■ ONETO
ACTOR ■ MEL ■ PERON
```

28

```
BEAM ■ ISLIP ■ PSST
LIRA ■ SCALA ■ ATTY
ONTHEROCKS ■ TRAP
CESAR ■ NEAT ■ RAGE
■ ■ LITER ■ ELOISE
CHOICE ■ ■ CLING ■
LINA ■ REMO ■ ASHES
AFT ■ PITCHER ■ TLC
NIHIL ■ TINA ■ HULA
■ ELIDE ■ REAPER
MAHLER ■ BANAL ■
ALOU ■ ALEC ■ SLOES
PLUS ■ WITHATWIST
LOSE ■ OTTER ■ ASTI
EWES ■ NEEDY ■ YEAR
```

29

```
JAPED ■ STEVE ■ UMP
ARENA ■ KALAMAZOO
GOODBYECOLUMBUS
SON ■ NEWT ■ ■ WEST
■ ■ PEWS ■ REMAKES
ALWAYS ■ CAMAY ■
LIRA ■ COLIN ■ FEE
AFAREWELLTOARMS
REP ■ LIDDY ■ ■ BOMP
■ ■ MOLES ■ ZEEMAN
BEWAILS ■ TINT ■
REAR ■ ■ LUNG ■ NEW
ARRIVEDERCIROMA
WINNEBAGO ■ NEVIL
LES ■ ENDOW ■ EXALT
```

30

```
ASAP ■ SAME ■ MOJOS
JUDO ■ ALEX ■ IRISH
ALAS ■ SOOT ■ SANTA
MUMSTHEWORD ■ REM
■ URI ■ RAE ■ IOU
THEMOMMYTRACK ■
RAY ■ DIDO ■ ELAINE
ILED ■ SKA ■ DSOS
OSWEGO ■ UPTO ■ HAT
■ IREMEMBERMAMA
COT ■ IND ■ NEE
ANN ■ SIERRAMADRE
BEECH ■ ROAN ■ DOOR
ATSEA ■ LAIC ■ OLEG
LOSES ■ EDDY ■ WEGO
```

31

```
CITE ■ PESCI ■ RAFT
ORES ■ LIMON ■ ERLE
MIAPHARAOH ■ STUN
ESS ■ AUEL ■ AWAKEN
THEEND ■ LALALA
■ SKIS ■ GENERIC
WORM ■ TIRADE ■ NNE
HAYES ■ MAT ■ SPARE
AHA ■ OPINES ■ EKES
TUNEFUL ■ SPAN ■
■ OXIDES ■ ASSAIL
PENTAD ■ TARA ■ SOU
LAIR ■ LEONSPHINX
UCLA ■ EMOTE ■ IDIO
SHES ■ SUPER ■ TEAR
```

32

```
VASE ■ FLORA ■ TET
IMUS ■ LAVER ■ SILO
DONTHAVEACOWMAN
ARS ■ AMIND ■ PEONY
LETITBE ■ BEARD ■
■ ROSE ■ SCANT ■
IRON ■ STORE ■ RES
TAKEADEEPBREATH
OWE ■ VILAS ■ NICE
■ WIELD ■ MAIN ■
CHEAT ■ COLDWAR
SHYER ■ RAISA ■ ALE
KEEPYOURSHIRTON
YENS ■ ALICE ■ CENT
ERA ■ FEDOR ■ ARES
```

33

T	A	D	■	C	R	A	W	■	I	S	O	M	E	R
A	L	I	■	A	I	D	E	■	D	E	V	A	N	E
M	A	S	S	B	O	O	K	■	L	E	A	N	T	O
A	M	M	O	S	■	R	I	L	E	Y	■	N	I	P
R	O	O	M	■	M	E	S	A	■	A	W	I	R	E
A	D	U	E	■	A	R	S	I	S	■	O	X	E	N
C	E	N	T	E	R	■	I	N	C	A	N	■	■	■
■	■	T	H	E	K	I	N	G	A	N	D	I	■	■
■	I	R	E	N	A	■	■	R	E	E	D	E	D	■
T	W	I	N	■	T	A	S	T	E	■	R	E	N	E
R	I	N	G	S	■	P	H	I	S	■	F	A	T	E
A	T	M	■	T	A	T	A	R	■	J	U	L	E	P
C	H	A	S	E	R	■	D	A	T	E	L	I	N	E
K	I	T	K	A	T	■	O	D	O	R	■	S	T	N
S	N	E	A	K	Y	W	E	E	K	■	T	E	D	■

34

E	R	E	C	T	S	■	S	L	A	G	■	G	A	P
N	U	C	L	E	I	■	A	U	T	O	R	A	C	E
C	E	R	I	U	M	■	S	T	O	R	E	S	U	P
■	■	■	U	P	T	O	T	H	E	M	I	N	U	T	E
■	■	■	O	O	O	■	■	■	■	L	O	P	E	■
H	A	D	I	N	M	E	M	O	R	Y	■	■	■	■
E	L	E	M	I	■	E	W	E	■	B	L	A	B	■
A	F	R	I	C	A	N	A	N	T	E	L	O	P	E
D	A	M	N	■	R	E	D	■	Y	O	U	S	E	■
■	■	■	G	R	E	E	K	L	E	T	T	E	R	■
O	H	I	O	■	■	■	O	U	S	■	■	■	■	■
F	R	E	N	C	H	P	R	O	N	O	U	N	■	■
L	O	R	R	A	I	N	E	■	A	R	R	O	W	S
U	N	D	E	R	L	I	E	■	T	E	N	N	I	S
B	O	S	■	T	O	N	K	■	E	S	S	E	N	E

35

R	A	M	P	■	D	O	R	Y	■	A	M	U	R
O	V	E	R	■	A	P	E	A	R	■	N	I	N	A
C	I	A	O	■	W	E	D	G	E	■	A	S	W	E
C	A	L	V	I	N	C	O	O	L	I	D	G	E	■
O	N	S	I	T	E	■	■	■	I	D	E	A	L	■
■	■	■	D	I	D	N	T	S	A	Y	M	U	C	H
A	C	H	E	S	■	O	R	A	N	■	G	O	O	■
I	R	A	S	■	B	R	A	N	T	■	R	E	M	O
D	U	N	■	L	U	S	T	■	M	U	S	E	D	■
A	N	D	W	H	E	N	H	E	D	I	D	■	■	■
■	C	L	E	A	N	■	■	E	R	I	C	A	S	■
H	E	D	I	D	N	T	S	A	Y	M	U	C	H	■
G	I	B	E	■	E	A	R	E	D	■	E	R	I	E
T	E	A	L	■	D	R	I	V	E	■	N	I	D	I
E	R	R	S	■	C	O	E	N	■	T	A	S	K	■

36

S	H	A	G	■	B	R	A	S	■	J	A	R	■
P	Y	L	E	■	R	I	T	A	■	L	U	B	E	S
U	P	A	N	D	A	D	A	M	■	E	L	E	N	A
D	E	S	E	R	V	E	■	A	N	T	I	L	O	G
■	■	■	R	O	O	■	■	R	E	H	A	B	■	■
P	E	C	A	N	S	■	L	I	S	A	■	O	P	S
A	M	A	T	E	■	B	O	T	T	L	E	D	U	P
L	A	N	E	■	S	A	G	A	S	■	P	I	T	A
M	I	D	D	L	E	T	O	N	■	R	H	E	T	T
S	L	Y	■	A	C	H	S	■	T	I	E	D	Y	E
■	■	C	A	R	T	S	■	E	L	M	■	■	■	■
S	P	A	N	I	S	H	■	T	R	E	E	T	O	P
O	U	I	J	A	■	E	V	E	S	D	R	O	P	S
O	R	N	O	T	■	B	I	L	E	■	A	M	E	S
■	L	S	U	■	A	P	E	R	■	L	E	N	T	■

37

B	I	N	D	■	F	A	R	R	■	F	A	T	S	O
O	T	O	E	■	O	B	O	E	■	A	H	E	A	D
A	S	I	F	■	R	E	B	A	■	R	O	A	L	D
R	E	D	L	E	T	T	E	R	D	A	Y	S	■	■
S	L	E	E	V	E	S	■	L	I	D	■	P	R	E
■	F	A	C	E	R	■	P	I	P	■	C	O	A	L
■	■	■	T	R	I	T	O	N	■	P	L	O	P	S
W	H	I	T	E	E	L	E	P	H	A	N	T	■	■
C	H	A	O	S	■	L	A	S	E	R	S	■	■	■
B	O	N	N	■	P	E	R	■	E	A	S	E	L	■
S	A	D	■	L	I	V	■	E	P	S	I	L	O	N
■	■	B	L	U	E	I	N	T	H	E	F	A	C	E
F	L	O	O	R	■	S	O	H	O	■	I	N	K	S
L	E	O	N	E	■	E	G	A	L	■	E	D	I	T
Y	O	K	E	D	■	D	O	N	E	■	S	S	N	S

38

S	H	A	H	■	S	W	A	T	■	E	L	C	I	D
T	E	R	I	■	W	A	D	E	■	P	I	A	N	O
E	R	I	N	■	A	R	A	L	■	I	B	S	E	N
T	R	A	D	I	N	G	P	L	A	C	E	S	■	■
■	■	■	U	N	D	A	T	E	D	■	R	E	V	S
R	A	M	■	T	I	M	E	R	S	■	I	L	I	E
E	R	A	■	E	V	E	R	■	Y	A	L	T	A	■
A	M	S	■	R	E	S	■	W	P	A	■	I	A	M
P	A	T	O	N	■	■	G	R	O	W	■	O	L	E
E	D	E	N	■	A	T	R	A	I	N	■	T	E	D
D	A	R	E	■	B	R	E	N	N	E	R	■	■	■
■	■	P	L	A	C	I	N	G	T	R	A	D	E	S
R	E	L	A	X	■	P	A	L	E	■	J	A	V	A
O	M	A	N	I	■	O	D	E	R	■	I	L	E	X
D	U	N	E	S	■	D	A	D	S	■	V	I	N	E

39

```
CRUZ █ HIST █ REBAS
LENO █ ERLE █ BRAVA
ADAR █ BOON █ INSET
RUBBERNECKS █ █ EMU
ECLAT █ OGEE █ TBAR
SEE █ SPRINGBOARD
█ █ █ GENT █ TALIA
CAPITA █ █ OUTLAY
UTURN █ POSH █ █ █
STRETCHLIMO █ USA
TIPS █ OREL █ TIGER
OTO █ ELASTICBAND
MUSER █ STIR █ ENSE
EDENS █ EREI █ ADEN
RESET █ SARD █ MAST
```

40

```
BESOT █ HAS █ VOID
ILICH █ SANE █ EBRO
BELLE █ WHININESS
█ GEORGESMILEY █
SINCERE █ ALLTIME
RACK █ ATALE █ INON
ICE █ SPIN █ PAGED
█ LOHENGRIN █ █
NIMOY █ AREA █ ISM
ODIN █ SALAD █ ASTI
MORGANS █ MULCHED
█ ABRAHAMBEAME █
ACCOMPANY █ ADAPT
LOLA █ UKES █ FIELD
POET █ PEW █ SALES
```

41

```
ASKS █ ELFIN █ PERU
LILT █ LORNE █ AXIS
IDEA █ APACE █ LEON
ALITTLEMADNESS █
SEGUE █ SENSES █
█ █ ERE █ ATRIA
ELM █ INTHESPRING
MEOW █ CREDO █ ANTE
ISWHOLESOME █ DOS
TENAM █ █ EAT █
█ █ TEASES █ VALUE
█ EVENFORTHEKING
AVIV █ AEIOU █ EMIR
DELE █ CUTIN █ RITE
ONER █ TRUCK █ STET
```

42

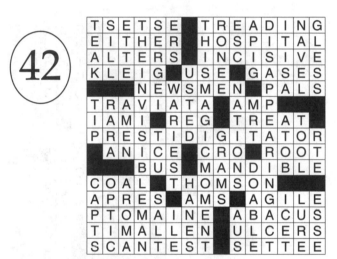

```
TSETSE █ TREADING
EITHER █ HOSPITAL
ALTERS █ INCISIVE
KLEIG █ USE █ GASES
█ NEWSMEN █ PALS
TRAVIATA █ AMP █
IAMI █ REG █ TREAT
PRESTIDIGITATOR
█ ANICE █ CRO █ ROOT
█ BUS █ MANDIBLE
COAL █ THOMSON █
APRES █ AMS █ AGILE
PTOMAINE █ ABACUS
TIMALLEN █ ULCERS
SCANTEST █ SETTEE
```

43

```
SNOW █ DRUB █ NON⁄
NOTA █ EERO █ OWES
CARRYABIG ⁄ SERB
CHARADES █ SHINDY
█ IKON █ THEE █
⁄AROUND █ MIRRORS
EVERT █ CAFE █ REL
MIAS █ BRUNT █ SIVA
ULM █ DRUM █ TIEUP
PASSION █ CANDLE⁄
█ COOS █ ALOE █
DISARM █ GROTTOES
IDOL █ ⁄TOTHERIBS
PYRE █ AREA █ ISAT
⁄LER █ BEDS █ PENS
```

44

```
STAGED █ DELMAR
TREETOP █ SELVAGE
PERSONALTRAINER
█ MOT █ STEAMY █ UNO
ROBES █ EGGON █ ADO
ELI █ OMNI █ ECLAT
DOC █ RATSO █ ITS
█ EMBELLISHER █
OXO █ YALTA █ ETA
SNEER █ TSAR █ AUG
TAR █ ANDIE █ PADRE
ETC █ SUAVER █ MMM
WEIGHTREDUCTION
EASIEST █ STOOLIE
DRESSY █ APOLLO
```

45

```
D O U B L E . . T W E N T Y
U S R I V E R . S H A K I E R
R O G A I N E . T A L E N T S
A L E S . . S H A W L S . .
N E S . C R O A T I A . E S S
. . . F A L L E N . A X L E
F A M . L I E F . G U S T A V
I W A S A . D B S . S E R I E
F A J I T A . A C T A . A N N
T K O S . B B K I N G . .
Y E R . T R I E S T E . T A B
. . S H A R D S . . H O R A
P R O K E D S . O S I E R E D
R E T I R E E . R A T R A C E
S I S T E R . . S I R H A N
```

46

```
H O I S T S . I H A D . J A B
M A N T R A . N A V E . A D O
O R D A I N . T I G E R C U B
. I R K . P E T . P O K E S
B R A V E M A R I N E R . .
L U N E . O Y L . E N E R O
A B E D . V I E . E D M O N D
S I X . R E N A R D S . Y E R
T E P E E S . G A L . M A D E
. S O T T O . U T E . A L G A
. Y A N K E E D O D G E R
S W A M I . N P R . V I I .
M E T A N G E L . C A S A B A
E R A . E L L A . A T O N A L
W E D . R O L Y . T E N T H S
```

47

```
. Z A P . T U B A . E S K E R
L O P E . A R A B . N O U S E
E D E L W E I S S . T H R O B
G I R L Y . . □ R O O T .
S A C . A B T . C R O . S E W
◇ C U T T E R . R I P . A R I
. S T R A T E G Y . W I N
E S M E . M U A N G . H A C K
C P A . D U M B N E S S .
H I D . I D A . A R C T I C ○
O L E . V A S . S S E . S O L
. L O V E △ . . N A O M I
L A V E R . S T A T E S M E N
A N E N T . L U C E . T E T E
C E R T S . O X E N . I R S .
```

48

```
C A N D I D . B A B S . S G T
A N Y O N E . M C I I . W O O
M E S S S T E W A R D . I R K
S W E A T E D . D E E P S E A
. G A N G . E M B A S S Y
A L D E N T E . M E E T S .
W O R S T E D . E S T A T E S
A G E . . . . E R A
R O S E T T A . D E S C A N T
. S C R E W . I N T A K E S
O B S C E N E . S C A N .
B E H E A D S . C A R D I A C
E L I . C R O S S S T I T C H
S L R . L I M E . E U D O R A
E A T . E L E E . S P A R E D
```

49

```
F A C E . L O D G E . N O S H
A T O P . A P I A N . O S T E
H O B O . M E A N T . M A R I
D I S C H A R G E . C I G A R
. H A S A ∠ F O R N E W S
P A L S Y . . R E A .
O R O . B A R T L E T T T P (ear)
P O K E . E R N I E . E R I N
(eye) W I T N E S S E S . O L E
. H I C . . A B N E R
J O H N P H I (heart) O U S A
A N A I S . S T U N S A I L S
P E R C . S L I T S . B A I T
A N T A . S A C R E . A G E E
N O E L . E S K E R . A O U T
```

50

```
B R E W . M O B Y . J A N E
O O Z E . O B I E . S I L A S
U A R E O N E B A C K T O S Q
T R A . N E S S . U I N T A S
. E S T E . A B L E
B L I M P S . R A I L Y A R D
A U D I E . M E R S . W O O
L C I R C L E C O M E S F U L
E R O . A S O N . L O U S E
D E M I J O H N . M E W L E D
. C I T Y . R E V S
S E V E N S . T I D E . E B B
P T I C K E T R O U N D T R I
A T L A S . O U T S . E N I D
S E E P . M E S A . Y A M S
```